NEWSPAPER CHINESE ABC
An Introductory Reader

Edited by Li Zhenjie
and Wang Shixun
Beijing Language Institute

Cheng & Tsui Company
Boston

Copyright © 1986 by the Beijing Language Institute

1998 Printing

All rights reserved. No part of this publication may be
reproduced or transmitted in any form or by any means,
electronic or mechanical, including photocopy, recording, or
any information storage or retrieval systems, without
permission in writing from the publisher.

Cheng and Tsui Company, Inc.
25 West Street
Boston, Massachusetts 02111-1268 USA

http://www.cheng-tsui.com

Library of Congress Cataloging in Publication Data:

Li Zhenjie and Wang Shixun
Newspaper Chinese ABC: An Introductory Reader
(C & T Asian Language Series)
I. Li Zhenjie and Wang Shixun II. Title III. Series
86-71549

Text ISBN 0-88727-059-X
Audio Tapes ISBN 0-88727-167-7

PUBLISHER'S NOTE

The Cheng & Tsui Company is pleased to announce the reprint of one of its central titles, **Newspaper Chinese ABC: An Introductory Reader**.

The C & T Asian Language Series is designed to publish and widely distribute quality language texts as they are completed by such leading institutions as the Beijing Language Institute, as well as other significant works in the field of Asian languages developed in the United States and elsewhere.

We welcome readers' comments and suggestions concerning the publications in this series. Please contact the following members of the editorial board:

Professor Shou-hsin Teng, Chief Editor
Dept. of Asian Languages and Literature
University of Massachusetts, Amherst, MA 01003

Professor Samuel Cheung
Dept. of East Asian Languages,
University of California, Berkeley, CA 94720

Professor Ying-che Li
Dept. of East Asian Languages,
University of Hawaii, Honolulu, HI 96822

Professor Timothy Light
Office of the President
Western Michigan University, Kalamazoo, MI 49008

Professor Stanley R. Munro
Dept. of East Asian Languages and Literature,
University of Alberta, Edmonton, Alberta, Canada

说 明

《报刊语言初阶》为汉语短训班"报刊阅读"课教材,大部分课文选自1982年《人民日报》和《新华社新闻稿》。每课前有若干范句,并配有注音和英译,以帮助学生更好地掌握中国报刊语言特点。课文附有英译,以备参考。全书共有报刊常见词语500条。本书也适合自学者使用。学完本书可初步掌握报刊基本句型和常见词语,阅读《人民日报》上的简单新闻报导。

编　者
1983年3月

第 一 课

一、范 句

1. 应 我 国 政府 邀请， 巴基斯坦 伊斯兰
   Yìng wǒ guó zhèngfǔ yāoqǐng Bājīsītǎn Yīsīlán
   共和国 总统 齐亚·哈克 上将 和 夫人 前来
   Gònghéguó zǒngtǒng Qíyà·Hākè shàngjiàng hé fūrén qiánlái
   进行 国事 访问。
   jìnxíng guóshì fǎngwèn

   General Mohammad Zia-ul-Haq, president of the Islamic Republic of Pakistan, and his wife arrived here on a state visit to China at the invitation of the Chinese Govermment.

2. 哈克 总统 今天 下午 乘 专机 到达 北京。
   Hākè zǒngtǒng jīntiān xiàwǔ chéng zhuānjī dàodá Běijīng

   President Zia-ul-Haq arrived in Beijing by special plane this affternoon.

3. 巴基斯坦 是 中国 的 友好 邻邦。
   Bājīsītǎn shì Zhōngguó de yǒuhǎo línbāng

   Pakistan is a friendly neighbour of China.

4. 我 国 政府 在 人民 大会堂 东门 外
   Wǒ guó zhèngfǔ zài Rénmín Dàhuìtáng dōngmén wài

		实现和平统一的方针政策　建议举行两党对等谈判实行第三次合作……………62
	阅读	叶委员长提出的九条方针政策大得人心……72
第六课		…………………………………………………75
	课文	五届人大五次会议在京开幕　彭真作关于宪法修改草案的报告…………………79
	阅读	中华人民共和国第四部宪法庄严诞生……86
第七课		…………………………………………………89
	课文	何东昌谈中国教育前景………………………92
	阅读	中国教育部长强调农村教育……………… 100
第八课		……………………………………………… 103
	课文	钱信忠再次强调计划生育………………… 106
	阅读	中国人口自然增长率下降………………… 113
第九课		……………………………………………… 116
	课文	一九八二年上半年安置二百四十万人就业……………………………………… 119
	阅读	受人们欢迎的劳动服务公司……………… 126
第十课		……………………………………………… 129
	课文	西藏领导干部赞扬党的民族政策………… 133
	阅读	西藏妇女的作用…………………………… 142
第十一课		……………………………………………… 144
	课文	中国国民经济出现协调发展的局面……… 147
	阅读	中国国民经济调整的初步成效…………… 155
第十二课		……………………………………………… 158
	课文	中国农民喜欢农业生产责任制…………… 161
	阅读	农业生产责任制改善了贫困地区农民的生活…………………………………… 171
词汇表		……………………………………………… 175

目　　录

第一课···1
　　课文　中国政府举行仪式欢迎巴基斯坦
　　　　　总统哈克···4
　　阅读（一）泰王国总理炳·廷素拉暖到达北京
　　　　　　　我国政府举行仪式热烈欢迎·······················11
　　　　（二）西德卡斯滕斯总统和夫人到达北京············12
第二课··15
　　课文　邓小平会见日本铃木首相······································18
　　阅读　中曾根首相表示要进一步发展日中
　　　　　友好关系···26
第三课··29
　　课文　中华人民共和国和美利坚合众国关于建立
　　　　　外交关系的联合公报···33
　　阅读（一）我国政府就中美建立外交关系发表声明····41
　　　　（二）胡耀邦谈中美关系···42
第四课··45
　　课文　我国外交部发言人发表声明　强烈谴责
　　　　　以色列屠杀巴勒斯坦平民···································48
　　阅读　安理会举行紧急会议一致通过决议　谴责
　　　　　以色列野蛮屠杀巴勒斯坦人的罪行···················56
第五课··59
　　课文　叶剑英委员长进一步阐明台湾回归祖国

1

广场　　举行　　隆重　　的　欢迎　　仪式。
guǎngchǎng jǔxíng lóngzhòng de huānyíng yíshì
The Chinese Government held a grand ceremony of welcome at a plaza east of the Great Hall of the People.

5. 广场　　　　上空　　飘扬着　　中巴　两国
Guǎngchǎng shàngkōng piāoyángzhe Zhōng-Bā liǎng guó
国旗。
guóqí
The national flags of China and Pakistan flew high above the plaza.

6. 欢迎　仪式　由　赵　紫阳　总理　主持。
Huānyíng yíshì yóu Zhào Zǐyáng zǒnglǐ zhǔchí
Premier Zhao Ziyang presided over the welcoming ceremony.

7. 少先队员　向　哈克　总统　和　夫人　献了
Shàoxiānduìyuán xiàng Hākè zǒngtǒng hé fūren xiànle
鲜花。
xiānhuā
Young pioneers presented president and his wife with bouquets.

8. 军乐队　奏　巴中　两国　国歌。
Jūnyuèduì zòu Bā-Zhōng liǎng guó guógē
The millitary band played the national anthems of Pakistan and China.

9. 哈克　总统　由　赵紫阳　　总理　陪同，
Hākè zǒngtǒng yóu Zhào Zǐyáng zǒnglǐ péitóng
检阅了　中国　人民　解放军　陆海空　三
jiǎnyuèle Zhōngguó Rénmín Jiěfàngjūn lù-hǎi-kōng sān

军 仪仗队。
jūn yínzhàngduì

Accompanied by Zhao Ziyang, president Haq reviewed a guard of honor made up of men from the three services of the Chinese People's Liberation Army.

10. 我 国 驻 巴基斯坦 大使 王 传斌 和 夫人
    Wǒ guó zhù Bājīsītǎn dàshǐ Wáng Chuánbīn hé fūren
    参加了 欢迎 仪式。
    cānjiāle huānyíng yíshì

Wang Chuanbin, Chinese ambassador to Pakistan, and his wife, attended the welcoming ceremony.

11. 随同 哈克 总统 来访 的 巴基斯坦 贵宾
    Suítóng Hākè zǒngtǒng láifǎng de Bājīsītǎn guìbīn
    出席了 欢迎 仪式。
    chūxíle huānyíng yíshì

The distinguished Pankistan guests who are accompanying president Haq on the visit, were present at the welcoming ceremony.

12. 宾 主 进行了 亲切 友好 的 交谈。
    Bīn-zhǔ jìnxíngle qīnqiè yǒuhǎo de jiāotán

The hosts and guests had a cordial and friendly conversation.

二、课　文

中国政府举行仪式欢迎巴基斯坦总统哈克

新华社北京 10 月 17 日电　应我国政府邀请，巴基斯坦伊斯兰共和国总统齐亚·哈克上将和夫人前来进行国事访问，今天下午乘专机到达北京。

巴基斯坦是中国的友好邻邦。哈克总统曾两次访华。今天下午四点三十分，我国政府在人民大会堂东门外广场举行隆重仪式，对哈克总统第三次来访表示热烈欢迎。广场上空飘扬着中巴两国国旗。

欢迎仪式由赵紫阳总理主持。当哈克总统和夫人乘车来到广场时，赵紫阳同他们热情握手，互致问候。少先队员向哈克总统和夫人献了鲜花。

欢迎仪式开始，军乐队奏巴中两国国歌。哈克总统由赵紫阳总理陪同，检阅了中国人民解放军陆海空三军仪仗队。随后，哈克总统同欢迎群众见面。二百多名少年儿童手舞花环彩带，纵情高呼："欢迎，欢迎，热烈欢迎！"哈克总统满面笑容，连连向群众招手。

国务委员兼外交部长黄华和夫人，外交部副部长吴学谦，我国驻巴基斯坦大使王传斌和夫人等，参加了欢迎仪式。

随同哈克总统来访的巴基斯坦联邦顾问委员会主席

赫瓦贾·穆罕默德·萨夫达尔，外交部长萨哈布扎达·雅各布·汗，驻中国大使巴蒂和夫人等出席了欢迎仪式。

欢迎仪式后，赵紫阳总理、哈克总统和夫人以及其他巴基斯坦贵宾步入人民大会堂。宾主进行了亲切友好的交谈。

(1982年)

三、生词

1. 政府　　　(名) zhèngfǔ　　　government
2. 仪式　　　(名) yíshì　　　　ceremony
3. 总统　　　(名) zǒngtǒng　　president
4. 应……邀请　　yīng…yāoqǐng　at the invitation of
5. 上将　　　(名) shàngjiàng　　general
6. 夫人　　　(名) fūren　　　　wife
7. 国事访问　　guóshì fǎngwèn　state visit
8. 专机　　　(名) zhuānjī　　　special plane
9. 邻邦　　　(名) línbāng　　　neighbour country
10. 曾　　　　(副) céng　　　　once
11. 隆重　　　(形) lóngzhòng　　grand; solemn
12. 主持　　　(动) zhǔchí　　　preside over
13. 少先队员　(名) shàoxiānduìyuán
　　　　　　　　　　　　　　　Young pioneer
14. 军乐队　　(名) jūnyuèduì　　military band
15. 奏　　　　(动) zòu　　　　　play
16. 国歌　　　(名) guógē　　　　national anthem
17. 陪同　　　(动) péitóng　　　accompany
18. 检阅　　　(动) jiǎnyuè　　　review

19.	仪仗队	（名）	yízhàngduǐ	guard of honour
20.	群众	（名）	qúnzhòng	the masses
21.	国务委员	（名）	guówù wěiyuán	State Councillor
22.	兼	（动）	jiān	hold two or more jobs concurrently
23.	外交部长	（名）	wàijiāo bùzhǎng	minister of foreign affairs
24.	副部长	（名）	fùbùzhǎng	vice-minister
25.	驻	（动）	zhù	halt; stay; be stationed
26.	大使	（名）	dàshǐ	ambassador
27.	随同	（动）	suítóng	be accompanying
28.	出席	（动）	chūxí	attend; be present
29.	贵宾	（名）	guìbīn	distinguished guest

专 名

1. 新华社　　　Xīnhuáshè　　Xinhua News Agency
2. 巴基斯坦伊斯兰共和国
　　　　　　　Bājīsītǎn Yīsīlán Gònghéguó
　　　　　　　the Islamic Republic of Pakistan
3. 齐亚·哈克　　Qíyà·Hākè　　人名(Zia-ul-Haq)
4. 赵紫阳　　　Zhào Zǐyáng　　人名
5. 黄华　　　　Huáng Huá　　人名
6. 吴学谦　　　Wú Xuéqiān　　人名
7. 王传斌　　　Wáng Chuánbīn　人名
8. 巴基斯坦联邦顾问委员会
　　　　　　　Bājīsītǎn Liánbāng Gùwèn Wěiyuánhuì
　　　　　　　the Federal Council of

Pakistan
9. 赫瓦贾·穆罕默德·萨夫达尔
   Hèwǎnjiǎ· Mùhànmòdé· Sāfūdáěr
   人名
10. 萨哈布扎达·雅各布·汗
    Sāhābùzhādá· Yǎgèbù· Hàn
    人名
11. 巴蒂   Bādì   人名

Translation

The Chinese Government Welcomes Pakistan President at Ceremony

Beijing, October 17 (Xinhua) General Mohammad Zia-ul-Haq, president of the Islamic Republic of Pakistan, and his wife Begum Haq arrived in Beijing by special plane this afternoon on a state visit to China at the invitation of the Chinese Government.

Pakistan is a friendly neighbour of China and President Haq has visited China twice before.

At 4:30 pm the Chinese Government held a grand ceremony at a plaza east of the Great Hall of the People, giving a red-carpet welcome to President Haq on his third visit to China. The national flags of China and Pakistan flew over the plaza.

Premier Zhao Ziyang presided over the ceremony. When President and Begum Haq drove to the plaza, Zhao Ziyang stepped forward to greet them with warm handshakes. Young pioneers presented President Haq and Begum Haq with bouquets.

The ceremony began with the military band playing the national anthems of Pakistan and China. Accompanied by Zhao Ziyang, President Haq reviewed a guard of honour of men from the three services of the Chinese People's Liberation Army.

Then, the President walked over to meet the welcomers. More than 200 children waved flowers and colourful streamers and shouted: "welcome, welcome, a warm welcome."

President Haq smiled and waved in acknowledgement.

Attending the welcoming ceremony were Huang Hua, State Councillor and Minister of Foreign Affairs, and his wife; Wu Xueqian, Wice-Minister of Foreign Affairs.

Also present were members of president's entourage: Khawaja Mohammad Safadar, Chairman of the Federal Council; Sahabzada Yaqub Khan, Minister for Foreign Affair; and Maqbool Ahmad Bhatty, Pakistan ambassador to China, and his wife.

After the ceremony, Premier Zhao Ziyan, President and Begum Haq, and other distinguished Pakistan guests filed into the Great Hall of the People.

The hosts and guests had a cordial conversation.

四、练　习

一、替换练习：

1. 应中国政府邀请，巴基斯坦伊斯兰共和国总统齐亚·哈克上将和夫人前来我国进行 | 国事 / 友好 / 正式 | 访问。

2. 哈克总统今天下午乘专机 | 到达 / 抵达 / 前往 / 回到 | 北京。

3. 哈克总统由赵紫阳总理陪同， | 检阅 / 游览 / 参观 / 访问 | 了

   | 中国人民解放军仪仗队。
   | 长城
   | 汽车制造厂
   | 西安

4. 随同来访的巴基斯坦贵宾 | 出席 / 参加 | 了 | 欢迎仪式 / 会谈 |。

5. 宾主双方 进行了亲切友好的 交谈/谈话。

二、选择适当的介词填入下列各句：

　　在　对　由　向　同

1. 应中国政府的邀请，巴基斯坦总统齐亚·哈克＿＿＿＿我国进行正式友好访问。
2. 中国政府＿＿＿＿人民大会堂东门外广场举行欢迎仪式。
3. 欢迎仪式＿＿＿＿国务院总理赵紫阳主持。
4. 赵紫阳总理＿＿＿＿哈克总统热情握手，互致问候。
5. 两名少先队员＿＿＿＿哈克总统和夫人献了鲜花。
6. 哈克总统满面笑容，＿＿＿＿欢迎群众见面，连连＿＿＿＿群众招手致意。

三、用指定的词语改写下列句子：

1. 中国政府邀请巴基斯坦总统来华进行国事访问。
　　　　　　　　　　　　　　　　（应……邀请）
2. 外交部副部长吴学谦陪同哈克总统离开北京前往西安访问。
　　　　　　　　　　　　　　　　（由……陪同）
3. 1982年12月，赵紫阳总理访问了非洲一些国家。
　　　　　　　　　　　　　　　（对……进行……）
4. 巴基斯坦驻华大使巴蒂和夫人出席了欢迎仪式。
　　　　　　　　　　　　　　（出席欢迎仪式的还有……）

四、熟悉下列词组：

1. 国事/友好/正式/非正式 访问

2. 举行 欢迎仪式/会谈/宴会/庆祝活动

3.
乘	飞机
	专机
	火车
	专车
	专列

4.
参加	欢迎仪式
出席	
主持	

5.
亲切友好的	交谈
	谈话
	会谈

五、阅 读

（一）

泰王国总理炳·廷素拉暖到达北京
我国政府举行仪式热烈欢迎

新华社北京 11 月 17 日电 泰王国总理炳·廷素拉暖上将应我国政府邀请前来进行正式友好访问，今天下午乘专机到达北京。

这是炳总理 1980 年 3 月就任总理以后，第二次来我国访问。

我国政府在人民大会堂东门外广场举行仪式欢迎炳总理。国务院总理赵紫阳主持了欢迎仪式。

广场上空飘扬着泰中两国国旗。当炳·廷素拉暖来到广场时，赵紫阳同他热情握手，表示欢迎。少先队员向炳总理献了鲜花。

军乐队奏两国国歌后，炳总理由赵总理陪同检阅了中国人民解放军三军仪仗队。200名少年儿童一边拍着手鼓一边跳舞，向泰国贵宾致意。

国务院副总理万里，外交部副部长吴学谦，中国驻泰国大使沈平等，出席了欢迎仪式。

出席欢迎仪式的还有随同炳总理来访的泰国副总理森·纳那空上将等高级官员以及泰国驻中国大使阿拉春·他纳蓬。

欢迎仪式后，赵紫阳同炳·廷素拉暖等贵宾在人民大会堂进行了亲切友好的谈话。

炳总理一行抵达北京时，吴学谦到机场迎接。

（1982年）

（二）

西德卡斯滕斯总统和夫人到达北京

新华社北京10月10日电 德意志联邦共和国总统卡尔·卡斯滕斯和夫人，应人大常委会和中国政府邀请前来进行国事访问，今天下午乘专机到达北京。

外交部副部长章文晋和夫人等到机场迎接。德意志联邦共和国驻中国大使修德也到机场迎接。

十年前，中国和德意志联邦共和国正式建立了外交关系。在两国建交十周年之际，卡斯滕斯总统到中国访问，这将进一步推动两国友好合作关系的发展。

今天，首都主要街道上空悬挂着彩旗。天安门广场上，两国国旗迎风飘扬。欢迎卡斯滕斯总统的正式仪式将于明天举行。

(1982年)

生 词

(一)

1. 正式　　（形）zhèngshì　　formal; official
2. 就任　　（动）jiùrèn　　take office; take up one's post
3. 高级官员　　gāojí guānyuán　high-ranking official
4. 一行　　（名）yīxíng　　a group travelling together; party
5. 抵达　　（动）dǐdá　　arrive; reach

(二)

6. 建交　　　jiànjiāo　　establish diplomatic relations
7. 推动　　（动）tuīdòng　　push forward; promote

专 名

(一)

1. 泰王国　　Tài Wángguó　　the Kingdom of Tailand
2. 炳·廷素拉暖

　　Bǐng·Tíngsùlānuǎn　人名

3. 万里　　　　Wàn Lǐ　　　　人名
4. 沈平　　　　Shěn Píng　　　人名
5. 森·纳那空
　　　　　　Sēn·Nànàkōng　　人名
6. 阿拉春·他纳蓬
　　　　　　Ālāchūn·Tānàpéng　人名

（二）

7. 德意志联邦共和国
　　　　　　Déyìzhì Liánbāng Gònghéguó
　　　　　　the Federal Republic of Germany
8. 卡尔·卡斯滕斯
　　　　　　Kǎěr· Kǎsīténgsī　人名
9. 人大常委会
　　　　　　Réndà Chángwěihuì　the Standing Committee of the National People's Congress
10. 章文晋　　Zhāng Wénjìn　　人名
11. 修德　　　Xiūdé　　　　　人名

问　题

1. 这条消息的内容是什么？
2. 泰国炳总理从前访问过中国吗？在什么时候？
3. 请你谈谈欢迎仪式的情况。
　　　　　×　　　　×　　　　×
4. 西德总统是应谁的邀请来华访问的？
5. 西德总统访华有什么意义？

第 二 课

一、范 句

1. 邓　小平　今天　上午　会见了　日本国　内阁
   Dèng Xiǎopíng jīntiān shàngwǔ huìjiànle Rìběnguó nèigé
   总理　大臣　铃木　善幸。
   zǒnglǐ dàchén Língmù Shànxìng

   Deng Xiaoping met with Japanese Prime Minister ZenKo Suzuki this morning.

2. 邓　小平　说："明天　是　实现　中 日
   Dèng Xiǎopíng shuō míngtiān shi shíxiàn Zhōng-Rì
   邦交　正常化　十　周年。"
   bāngjiāo zhèngchánghuà shí zhōunián

   Deng Xiaoping said: "Tomrrow will be the 10th anniversary of normalization of diplomatic relation between China and Japan."

3. 9 月 29 日 是 中 日 两 国 人民 值得
   Jiǔ yuè èrshíjiǔ rì shi Zhōng-Rì liǎng guó rénmín zhíde
   纪念 的 日子。
   jìniàn de rìzi

   September 29 is worth celebrating by the people of China and Japan.

4. 铃木　首相　　访问　中国　是　很　有
   Língmù shǒuxiàng fǎngwèn Zhōngguó shì hěn yǒu
   意义　的　事情。
   yìyì de shìqing

   Prime Minister Suzuki's China visit is of great significance.

5. 他　感谢　铃木　首相　为　中　日　邦交
   Tā gǎnxiè Língmù shǒuxiàng wèi Zhōng-Rì bāngjiāo
   正常化　　所　作　的　贡献。
   zhèngchánghuà suǒ zuò de gòngxiàn

   He thanked Prime Minister Suzuki's for his contributions to the normalization of Sino-Japanese diplomatic relations.

6. 他　也　感谢　一贯　从事　中　日　友好　的
   Tā yě gǎnxiè yīguàn cóngshì Zhōng-Rì yǒuhǎo de
   日本　各界　人士。
   Rìběn gèjiè rénshì

   He also thanked the persons of various Japanese circles working for friendship between China and Japan.

7. 中　日　两　国　人民　要　世世代代　友好
   Zhōng-Rì liǎng guó rénmín yào shìshì-dàidài yǒuhǎo
   下去。
   xiàqu

   The Chinese and Japanese people want to be friendly to each other from generation to generation.

8. 他　重申　发展　同　日本　的　关系　是
   Tā chóngshēn fāzhǎn tóng Rìběn de guānxi shì
   中国　的　长期　国策。
   Zhōngguó de chángqī guócè

He reiterated that to develop its relations with Japan is the long-term basic policy of China.

9. 铃木　首相　祝贺　中共　十二大　取得
   Língmù shǒuxiàng zhùhè Zhōnggòng Shí'èrdà qǔdé
   成功。
   chénggōng
   Prime-Minister Suzuki congratulated on the success of the 12th National Congress of the Communist Party of China.

10. 邓　小平　对　铃木　首相　的　祝贺　表示
    Dèng Xiǎopíng duì Língmù shǒuxiàng de zhùhè biǎoshì
    感谢。
    gǎnxiè
    Deng Xiaoping thanked the Prime Minister for his congratulations.

11. 我们　的　政策　在　十二大　得到了　确认。
    Wǒmen de zhèngcè zài Shí'èrdà dédàole quèrèn
    Our policies were affirmed at the 12th National Congress.

12. 我们　让　年轻　一些　的　同志　担任
    Wǒmen ràng niánqīng yīxiē de tóngzhì dānrèn
    第一线　工作。
    dìyīxiàn gōngzuò
    We have allowed younger comrades to take up "front-line" posts.

13. 我们　党　的　中央　委员会　里　60　岁
    Wǒmen dǎng de zhōngyāng wěiyuánhuì lǐ liùshí suì
    以下　的　同志　占　很　大　的　比例。
    yǐxià de tóngzhì zhàn hěn dà de bǐlì

Comrades under 60 have made up a fairly big percentage of the members of our Party Central Committee.

14. 邓 小平 和 铃木 还 就 一些 国际
    Dèng Xiǎopíng hé Língmù hái jiù yīxiē guójì
    问题 进行了 交谈。
    wèntí jìnxíngle jiāotán

    Deng Xiaoping and Suzuki also exchanged views on a number of international issues.

15. 会见 时 在座 的 有 国务 委员 兼
    Huìjiàn shí zàizuò de yǒu guówù wěiyuán jiān
    外长 黄华、 外交部 副部长 吴 学谦。
    wàizhǎng HuángHuá wàijiāobù fùbùzhǎng Wú Xuéqiān

    Present were Chinese State Councillor and Foreign Minister Huan Hua, Vice-Foreign Minister Wu Xueqian.

二、课 文

邓小平会见日本铃木首相

新华社北京9月28日电 邓小平今天上午在人民大会堂会见了日本国内阁总理大臣铃木善幸。会见时，邓小平说，明天是实现中日邦交正常化十周年，是两国人民值得纪念的日子。铃木首相在这个时候访问我国是很有意义的事情。他感谢田中、大平前首相和铃木首相、樱内外务大臣为两国邦交正常化所作出的贡献，同时也感谢一贯从事中日友好、为两国邦交正常化作出贡献的日本各界人士。

邓小平说，中日关系有许多话可说，概括成一句话就是，中日两国人民要世世代代友好下去。他重申发展同日本的关系是中国的长期国策。

铃木首相祝贺中共十二大取得成功。邓小平对此表示感谢。他说，十一届三中全会以来所制定的政策，在十二大得到了确认。最近几年，我们做了一件很重要的事，就是让年轻一些的同志担任第一线工作。可以说，我们的政策连续性的问题已经解决了。现在，我们党的中央委员会里60岁以下的同志占很大比例，以后还要加大这个比例，四五十岁的人要多一些。

邓小平和铃木还就一些国际问题进行了交谈。

随同铃木首相来访的樱内义雄、池田行彦、柳谷谦介等，日本驻中国大使鹿取泰卫，参加了会见。

会见时在座的有国务委员兼外长黄华，外交部副部长吴学谦，中国驻日本大使宋之光等。

(1982年)

三、生 词

1. 会见　　（动）huìjiàn　　　　meet
2. 内阁　　（名）nèigé　　　　　cabinet
3. 总理大臣（名）zǒnglǐ dàchén　prime minister
4. 邦交　　（名）bāngjiāo　　　diplomatic relation
5. 正常化　（动）zhèngchánghuà normalization

6.	周年	(名)	zhōunián	anniversary
7.	值得	(动)	zhídé	be worth
8.	纪念	(动)	jìniàn	commemorate; mark
9.	首相	(名)	shǒuxiàng	prime minister
10.	意义	(名)	yìyì	meaning; significance
11.	前(首相)		qián(shǒuxiàng)	former (prime minister)
12.	外务大臣	(名)	wàiwù dàchén	minister of foreign affairs
13.	贡献	(名、动)	gòngxiàn	contribution
14.	一贯	(形)	yīguàn	consistent; persistent
15.	从事	(动)	cóngshì	go in for; be engaged in
16.	各界		gèjiè	all walks of life; all circles
17.	人士	(名)	rénshì	personage; public figure
18.	概括	(动)	gàikuò	summarize; generalize; briefly
19.	世世代代		shìshì-dàidài	form generation to generation
20.	重申	(动)	chóngshēn	reiterate; reaffirm
21.	国策	(名)	guócè	national policy; basic policy of a state
22.	祝贺	(动)	zhùhè	congratulate
23.	届	(量)	jiè	(measure word)
24.	制定	(动)	zhìdìng	formulate
25.	政策	(名)	zhèngcè	policy
26.	确认	(动)	quèrèn	affirm
27.	担任	(动)	dānrèn	hold the post of
28.	第一线	(名)	dìyīxiàn	front-line
29.	连续性	(名)	liánxùxìng	continuity

30. 中央委员会
　　　　　　　zhōngyāng wěiyuánhuì
　　　　　　　Central Committee
31. 占　　　（动）zhàn　　　make up
32. 比例　　（名）bǐlì　　　percentage
33. 就　　　（介）jiù　　　on
34. 国际　　（名）guójì　　international
35. 在座　　　　　zàizuò　　be present (at a meeting, banquet, etc.)

专　名

1. 邓小平　　　Dèng Xiǎopíng　　人名
2. 日本国　　　Rìběnguó　　　　Japan
3. 铃木善幸　　Língmù Shànxìng　人名
4. 田中　　　　Tiánzhōng　　　　人名
5. 大平　　　　Dàpíng　　　　　人名
6. 樱内义雄　　Yīngnèi Yìxióng　人名
7. 十一届三中全会
　　　　　　Shíyī Jiè Sānzhōng Quánhuì
　　　　　　the Third Plenary Session of the 11th Party Committee
8. 池田行彦　　Chítián Xíngyàn　人名
9. 柳谷谦介　　Liǔgǔ Qiānjiè　　人名
10. 鹿取泰卫　　Lùqǔ Tàiwèi　　　人名
11. 宋之光　　　Sòng Zhīguāng　　人名

Translation

Deng Xiaoping Meets Japanese Prime Minister Zenko Suzuki

Beijing, September 28 (Xinhua)— Deng Xiaoping met with Japanese Cabinet Prime Minister Zenko Suzuki at the Great Hall of the People here this morning.

Deng Xiaoping said, tomorrow will be the 10th anniversary of the normalization of diplomatic relations between China and Japan, and it's worth celebrating. Prime Minister Suzuki's China visit at this time is of great significance. He thanked former Japanese Prime Minister Kakuei Tanaka, the late Prime Minister Masayoshi Ohira, Prime Minister Zenko Suzuki and Minister of Foreign Affairs Yoshio Sakurauchi for their contributions to the normalization of Sino-Japanese diplomatic relations. He also thanked the persons of various Japanese circles working for friendship between China and Japan and for the normalization of diplomatic relations.

"There are many words to say about Sino-Japanese relations. They can be summarized in one sentence, that is, the Chinese and Jepanese people want to be friendly to each other from generation to generation," Deng Xiaoping stated. He reiterated that to develop its relations with Japan is the long-term basic policy of China.

Prime Minister Zenko Suzuki congratulated on the success of the 12th National Congress of the Communist Party of China. Deng Xiaoping thanked the Prime Minister for his congratulations. He said, the policies formulated since the third Plenum of the 11th Central Committee were affirmed at the 12th National Congress. One thing of vital significance we have done in recent years is to allow younger comrades to take up "front-line" posts. It can be said that the continuity of our policy has been solved. Now, comrades under 60 have made up a fairly big percentage of the members of our Party Central Committee, and the percentage will grow in the future with the addition of more persons in their 40s and 50s.

Deng Xiaoping and Zenko Suzuki also exchanged views on a number of international issues.

Present at the meeting were Yoshio Sakurauchi, Yukikiko Ikeda and Kensoke Yanagiya who are accompanying the Prime Minister on the visit, and Japanese ambassador to China Yasue Katori.

Present were also Chinese State Councillor and Foreign Minister Hung Hua, Vice-Foreign Minister Wu Xueqian and Chinese ambassador to Japan Song Zhiguang.

四、练 习

一、替换练习：

1. 邓小平今天上午会见了 [日本内阁总理大臣铃木善幸 / 朝鲜民主主义人民共和国主席金日成 / 巴基斯坦总统齐亚·哈克将军]。

2. 9月29日是中日两国 [人民值得纪念 / 邦交正常化] 的日子。

3. 中国领导人重申 [发展同日本的关系 / 加强同第三世界的团结 / 反对霸权主义] 是中国的长期国策。

4. 邓小平对 [铃木首相的祝贺 / 日本各界人士的努力 / 外国朋友的支持] 表示感谢。

5. 两国领导人就 [一些国际 / 双边关系 / 共同关心的] 问题进行了交谈。

二、把下列词语分别填入各句:
　　　　进行　　制定　　会见　　值得
　　　　随同　　从事　　在座　　重申

1. 邓小平同志今天上午在人民大会堂 _____ 了日本首相铃木善幸。
2. 实现中日邦交正常化是一件两国人民 _____ 纪念的大事。
3. 邓小平对一贯 _____ 中日友好的日本各界人士表示感谢。
4. 中国领导人 _____ 发展同日本的关系是中国的长期国策。
5. 邓小平说,十一届三中全会以来所 _____ 的政策,在十二大得到了确认。
6. 两国领导人还就一些国际问题 _____ 了交谈。
7. _____ 铃木首相来访的樱内外相参加了会见。
8. 会见时 _____ 的有国务委员兼外长黄华。

三、用指定的词语改写下列句子:
1. 会见时,邓小平同铃木首相还谈到了一些国际问题。
　　　　　　　　　　　　　　　　　　(就……)
2. 他感谢一贯从事中日友好,为两国邦交正常化作出贡献的日本各界人士。　(表示……)
3. 我们党的中央委员会里60岁以下的同志比例很大。
　　　　　　　　　　　　　　　　　　(占……)
4. 国务委员兼外长黄华、外交部副部长吴学谦会见时在座。
　　　　　　　　　　　　　　　　　　(在座的有……)

四、熟悉下列词组:

1.	中日邦交 两国关系 双边关系	正常化		2.	前	首相 总统 总理	

3.	一贯	从事 坚持 主张 认为		4.	表示	感谢 祝贺 满意 赞成 反对	

5.	制定	政策 方针 计划 法律		6.	担任	第一线 基层 领导 重要	工作

五、阅　读

中曽根首相打电话给赵紫阳总理表示

要进一步发展日中友好关系

赵紫阳对中曽根就任内阁总理大臣表示衷心祝贺

新华社北京12月1日电　本报记者从外交部获悉：
日本新任首相中曽根康弘今天下午五时三十分从东京打

电话给中国总理赵紫阳,表示要进一步发展日中友好关系。他说,发展日中两国良好的、稳定的关系,是日本外交的重要支柱。

外交部的人士说,赵紫阳总理对于中曾根首相特地打来电话表示感谢,他对中曾根康弘就任日本国内阁总理大臣表示衷心的祝贺。

据悉,中曾根在电话中还转达了铃木善幸对赵紫阳的问候。中曾根说,铃木首相对于不久前他在中国访问期间受到的热情款待表示感谢。赵紫阳请中曾根转达他对铃木的问候。

赵紫阳在电话中对中曾根说,今年是中日邦交正常化十周年。十年来,两国关系的发展是令人满意的。他希望,在中曾根康弘就任首相以后,两国的友好合作关系能够在现在的基础上取得进一步的发展。赵紫阳表示,中国政府愿意同中曾根首相领导下的日本政府为此目的而共同努力。

外交部人士提供的情况说,中曾根首相在电话交谈中表示,他与赵总理对发展日中关系的看法是一致的。他说,两国关系具有天时地利人和的良好条件。他希望今后要进一步发展日中友好关系和两国经济合作关系。

(1982年)

生　词

1. 衷心　　　(形) zhōngxīn　　wholehearted; heartfelt

2. 稳定　　　（形）wěndìng　　　stable; steady
3. 支柱　　　（名）zhīzhù　　　pillar; prop
4. 转达　　　（动）zhuǎndá　　　pass on; convey
5. 款待　　　（动）kuǎndài　　　treat cordially; entertain
6. 提供　　　（动）tígōng　　　provide; supply; offer
7. 一致　　　（形）yīzhì　　　identical; unanimous
8. 天时　　　（名）tiānshí　　　time-liness; opportunity
9. 地利　　　（名）dìlì　　　favourable geographical position; topographical advantages
10. 人和　　　（名）rénhé　　　support of the people; unity and coordination within one's own ranks

专　名

中曾根康弘　Zhōngzēnggēn Kānghóng　　　人名

问　题

1. 日本新任首相中曾根给谁打了电话？表示了什么意见？
2. 赵紫阳总理在电话中谈了什么？
3. 中曾根赞同赵紫阳关于中日关系的看法吗？
4. 他们在电话中还谈了什么？
5. 你能谈谈什么叫"天时、地利、人和"吗？

第 三 课

一、范 句

1. 中华　　人民　　共和国　　和　美利坚　　合众国
   Zhōnghuá Rénmín Gònghéguó hé Měilìjiān Hézhòngguó
   决定　自　一　九　七　九　年　一月　一　日　起　建立
   juédìng zì yī jiǔ qī jiǔ nián yīyuè yī rì qǐ jiànlì
   外交　关系。
   wàijiāo guānxi

   The People's Republic of China and the United States of America have decided to establish diplomatic relations as of January 1. 1979.

2. 中　美　建　交　公报　提前　于　今天　上　午
   Zhōng-Měi jiàn jiāo gōngbào tíqián yú jīntiān shàngwǔ
   公布。
   gōngbù

   The joint communique on the establishment of diplomatic relations between China and U·S was made known in advance on tody's morning.

3. 美　利　坚　　合　众　国　　承　认　　中华　人　民
   Měilìjiān Hézhòngguó chéngrèn Zhōnghuá Rénmín
   共和国　　政府　是　中国　的　唯一　合法
   Gònghéguó zhèngfǔ shi Zhōngguó de wéiyī héfǎ

政府。
zhèngfǔ

The United States of America recognizes the Government of the People's Republic of China as the sole legal Government of China;

4. 美国 人民 将 同 台湾 人民 保持 非官方 关系。
Měiguó rénmín jiāng tóng Táiwān rénmín bǎochí fēi-guānfāng guānxi

The people of the United States will maintain unoffical relations with the people of Taiwan.

5. 中华 人民 共和国 和 美利坚 合众国 重申 上海 公报 中 的 各项 原则。
Zhōnghuá Rénmín Gònghéguó hé Měilìjiān Hézhòngguó chóngshēn Shànghǎi Gōngbào zhong de gè xiàng yuánzé

The People's Republic of China and the United States of America reaffirm the principles in the Shanghai Communique.

6. 双方 都 希望 减少 国际 军事 冲突 的 危险。
Shuāngfāng dōu xīwàng jiǎnshǎo guójì jūnshì chōngtū de wēixiǎn

Both wish to reduce the danger of international military conflict.

7. 任何 一方 都 不 应该 在 亚洲—太平洋 地区 谋求 霸权。
Rènhé yīfāng dōu bù yīnggāi zài Yàzhōu-Tàipíngyáng dìqū móuqiú bàquán

Neither should seek hegemony in the Asia-Pacific region.

8. 每 一方 都 反对 任何 其它 国家 建立
   Měi yīfāng dōu fǎnduì rènhé qítā guójiā jiànlì
   这种 霸权。
   zhèzhǒng bàquán
   Each is opposed to establish such hegemony by any other country;

9. 任何 一方 都 不 准备 代表 任何 第三方
   Rènhé yīfāng dōu bù zhǔnbèi dàibiǎo rènhé dìsānfāng
   进行 谈判。
   jìnxíng tánpàn.
   Neither is prepared to negotiate on behalf of any third party;

10. 任何 一方 都 不 准备 同 对方 达成
    Rènhé yīfāng dōu bù zhǔnbèi tóng duìfāng dáchéng
    针对 其他 国家 的 协议 或 谅解。
    zhēnduì qítā guójiā de xiéyì huò liàngjiě
    Neither is prepared to enter into agreement or understanding with the other directed at other states.

11. 美利坚 合众国 政府 承认 中国 的 立场。
    Měilìjiān Hézhòngguó zhèngfǔ chéngrèn Zhōngguó de lìchǎng
    The Government of the United States of America acknowledges the Chinese position.

12. 台湾 是 中国 的 一 部分。
    Táiwān shi Zhōngguó de yī bùfen
    Taiwan is part of China.

13. 中　美　关系　　正常化　　符合　中国　人民
　　 Zhōng-Měi guānxi zhèngchánghuà fúhé Zhōngguó rénmín
　　 和　美国　人民　的　利益。
　　 hé Měiguó rénmín de lìyì

The normalization of Sino-America relation is in the interest of the Chinese and American peoples.

14. 中　美　关系　　正常化　　有助于　　亚洲　和
　　 Zhōng-Měi guānxi zhèngchánghuà yǒuzhùyú Yàzhōu hé
　　 世界　的　和平　事业。
　　 shìjiè de hépíng shìyè

The normalization of Sino-America relation contributes to the cause of peace in Asia and the world.

15. 中　华　　人民　共和国　　和　美利坚　合　众　国
　　 Zhōnghuá Rénmín Gònghéguó hé Měilìjiān Hézhòngguó
　　 于　一　九　七　九　年　三月　一　日　互　派
　　 yú yī jiǔ qī jiǔ nián sānyuè yī rì hù pài
　　 大使。
　　 dàshǐ

The People's Republic of China and the United States of America exchanged Ambassadors on March 1, 1979.

二、课　文

中华人民共和国和美利坚合众国
关于建立外交关系的联合公报

新华社北京 12 月 16 日电　中华人民共和国和美利坚合众国决定自一九七九年一月一日起建立外交关系。经双方商定，中美建交联合公报提前于今天上午公布。联合公报的全文如下：

中华人民共和国和美利坚合众国关于建立外交关系的联合公报

一九七九年一月一日

中华人民共和国和美利坚合众国商定自一九七九年一月一日起互相承认并建立外交关系。

美利坚合众国承认中华人民共和国政府是中国的唯一合法政府。在此范围内，美国人民将同台湾人民保持文化、商务和其他非官方关系。

中华人民共和国和美利坚合众国重申上海公报中双方一致同意的各项原则，并再次强调：

——双方都希望减少国际军事冲突的危险。

——任何一方都不应该在亚洲——太平洋地区以及世界上任何地区谋求霸权，每一方都反对任何其他国家或国家集团建立这种霸权的努力。

——任何一方都不准备代表任何第三方进行谈判，也不准备同对方达成针对其他国家的协议或谅解。

——美利坚合众国政府承认中国的立场，即只有一个中国，台湾是中国的一部分。

——双方认为，中美关系正常化不仅符合中国人民和美国人民的利益，而且有助于亚洲和世界的和平事业。

中华人民共和国和美利坚合众国将于一九七九年三月一日互派大使并建立大使馆。

(1978 年)

三、生词

1. 外交关系		wàijiāo guānxi	diplomatic relations
2. 联合公报		liánhé gōngbào	joint communique
3. 决定	（动）	juédìng	decide; resolve
4. 商定	（动）	shāngdìng	decide through consultation; agree
5. 提前	（动）	tíqián	shift to an earlier date; in advance
6. 公布	（动）	gōngbù	publish; announce
7. 全文		quánwén	full text
8. 承认	（动）	chéngrèn	give diplomatic recognition; recognize
9. 唯一	（形）	wéiyī	sole
10. 合法	（形）	héfǎ	legal
11. 范围	（名）	fànwéi	limits
12. 保持	（动）	bǎochí	keep; maintain
13. 文化	（名）	wénhuà	culture

14.	商务	（名）	shāngwù	commerical affairs
15.	官方	（名）	guānfāng	official
16.	强调	（动）	qiángdiào	stress; emphasize
17.	减少	（动）	jiǎnshǎo	reduce
18.	军事冲突		jūnshì chōngtū	military conflict
19.	谋求	（动）	móuqiú	seek; strive for
20.	集团	（名）	jítuán	group
21.	谈判	（动）	tánpàn	negotiate
22.	对方	（名）	duìfāng	the other side; the other party
23.	达成	（动）	dáchéng	reach (agreement)
24.	针对	（动）	zhēnduì	be directed against
25.	协议	（名）	xiéyì	agreement
26.	谅解	（名、动）	liàngjiě	understanding; understand
27.	即	（动）	jí	be; mean
28.	符合	（动）	fúhé	accord with
29.	利益	（动）	lìyì	benefit; interest
30.	有助于		yǒuzhùyú	contribute to
31.	和平事业		hépíng shìyè	the cause of peace
32.	派	（动）	pài	send; dispatch
33.	大使馆	（名）	dàshǐguǎn	embassy

专　名

1. 中华人民共和国　Zhōnghuá Rénmín Gònghéguó
   the People's Republic of China

2. 美利坚合众国　Měilìjiān Hézhòngguó
　　　　　　　　　the United States of America
3. 台湾　　　　　Táiwān　省名
4. 上海公报　　　Shànghǎi Gōngbào
　　　　　　　　　Shanghai Communique

Establishment of Diplomatic Relations Between P.R.C. and U.S.A.

Beijing December 26 (Xinhua) The People's Republic of China and the United States of America have decided to establish diplomatic relations as of Jaunary 1, 1979. It was agreed upon through consultations between the two sides that the joint communique on the establishment of diplomatic relations was made known in advance on today's morning. The full text of the communique reads as follows:

Joint Communique on the Establishment of
Diplomatic Relations Between the
People's Republic of China and the
United States of America
January 1, 1979

The People's Republic of China and the United States of

America have agreed to recognized each other and to establish diplomatic relations as of January 1, 1979.

The United States of America recognizes the Government of the People's Republic of China as the sole legal Government of China. Within this context, the people of the United States will maintain cultural, commercial and other unofficial relations with the people of Taiwan.

The People's Republic of China and the United States of America reaffirm the principles agreed on by the two sides in the Shanghai Communique and emphasize once again that:

—Both wish to reduce the danger of international military conflict.

—Neither should seek hegemony in the Asia-Pacific region or in any other region of the world and each is opposed to efforts by any other country or group of countries to establish such hegemony.

—Neither is prepared to negotiate on behalf of any third party or enter into agreements or understandings with the other directed at other states.

—The Government of the United States of America acknowledges the Chinese position that there is but one China and Taiwan is part of China.

—Both believe that normalization of Sino-American relations is not only in the interest of the Chinese and American peoples but also contributes to the cause of peace in Asia and the world.

The People's Republic of China and the United States of America will exchange Ambassadors and establish Embassies on March 1, 1979.

四、练 习

一、替换练习：

1. 中华人民共和国和美利坚合众国 [商定／决定] 自一九七九年一月一日 [起／开始] 互相承认并建立 [外交关系／大使级外交关系]。

2. 美利坚合众国承认 [中华人民共和国／台湾] 是 [中国唯一合法政府／中国的一部分]。

3. 中华人民共和国和美利坚合众国 [重申／再次强调] 上海公报中双方一致同意的各项原则。

4. 任何一方都不准备同 [对方／另一方] 达成针对 [其他国家／第三方] 的协议和谅解。

5. 中美关系正常化不仅符合中国人民和美国人民的 |利益/愿望|，而且 |有助于/有利于| 亚洲和世界的和平事业。

二、用指定的词语改写下列句子：
1. 中华人民共和国和美利坚合众国商定自1979年1月1日起互相承认并建立外交关系。　　　　（经……商定）
2. 中华人民共和国政府于1978年12月16日发表了关于中美建立外交关系的声明。　　　　　　（就……发表）
3. 西德总统十月十一日开始对中国进行为期一周的国事访问。　　　　　　　　　　　　　　（自……起）
4. 美利坚合众国政府承认中国关于只有一个中国，台湾是中国的一部分的立场。　　　　　　（即……）

三、把下列词语分别填入各句：
　　　商定　承认　强调　谈判
　　　针对　谋求　符合　信守

1. 中国政府发表声明，再次_____，解决台湾归回祖国、完成国家统一的方式，这完全是中国的内政。
2. 不_____台湾是中国的一部分，就不能同中国建立外交关系。
3. 双方_____自一九八〇年七月起互派留学生,扩大文化交流。
4. 美国政府应该_____中美建交公报的原则，停止向台湾出售武器。
5. 不久前，美国和日本就两国贸易问题进行了_____。
6. 我们决不在世界上任何地区_____霸权，也反对任何其他国家这样做。

7. 中国不打"美国牌",也不打"苏联牌"。我们同一个国家发展正常的国家关系不是_____其他国家的。

8. 中美关系正常化不仅 _____ 两国人民的利益,而且有利于维护世界和平与稳定。

四、把下列介词填入各句:

自　于　同　为　以

1. 中美建交联合公报提前_____十二月十六日上午公布。

2. 巴基斯坦总统_____10月17日起对中国进行正式友好访问。

3. 美国承认中华人民共和国政府是中国的唯一合法政府。在此范围内,美国人民将_____台湾人民保持文化、商务等非官方关系。

4. 任何一方都不准备_____对方达成针对第三方的协议和谅解。

5. 只有_____中美建交公报的各项原则作为基础,中美两国关系才能得到发展。

6. 胡耀邦同志_____法共领导人进行了诚恳、坦率、友好的会谈。

7. 他在会见时表示,今后要_____加强两党关系而继续努力。

五、熟悉下列词组：

1. 发表｜公报
　　　　声明
　　　　谈话
　　　　社论
　　　　文章

2. 提前｜公布
　　　　宣布
　　　　实现
　　　　完成

3. 建立｜外交关系
　　　　共和国
　　　　新政权
　　　　联系

4. 谋求｜霸权
　　　　特权
　　　　利益
　　　　解决办法

5. 达成｜协议
　　　　协定
　　　　谅解
　　　　一致意见

6. 实现｜两国关系正常化
　　　　领导班子年轻化
　　　　四个现代化
　　　　五年计划

五、阅　读

（一）

就中美两国建立外交关系
我国政府发表声明

新华社北京 12 月 16 日电 中华人民共和国政府

今天就中美两国建立外交关系发表一项声明，重申台湾是中国的一部分。解决台湾归回祖国、完成国家统一的方式，这完全是中国的内政。

声明说：中华人民共和国和美利坚合众国自一九七九年一月一日起互相承认并建立外交关系，从而结束了两国关系的长期不正常状态。这是中美两国关系中的历史性事件。

众所周知，中华人民共和国政府是中国的唯一合法政府，台湾是中国的一部分。台湾问题曾经是阻碍中美两国实现关系正常化的关键问题。根据上海公报的精神，经过中美双方的共同努力，现在这个问题在中美两国之间得到了解决，从而使中美两国人民热切期望的关系正常化得以实现。至于解决台湾归回祖国、完成国家统一的方式，这完全是中国的内政。

(1978年)

(二)

胡耀邦谈中美关系

胡耀邦同志在中国共产党第十二次全国代表大会上就我国同美国的关系作了说明。

他说：中美两国自一九七九年建立外交关系以来，发展了符合两国人民利益的关系。我们一贯希望把这种关系发展下去，认为这对两国人民和世界和平都是有益的。可是两国关系中一直存在着阴影。这是因为，美国虽然承认中华人民共和国政府是中国唯一的合法政府，只有一个中国，台湾是中国的一部分，但是又通过了一个违反两国建交公报原则的"与台湾关系法"，继续向台湾出售武器，把台湾作为一个独立的政治实体对待。中国政府多次声明，这是侵犯中国主权、干涉中国内政的行为。中美两国政府经过将近一年的谈判，不久前发表联合公报，对美国向台湾出售武器问题作出了分步骤直到最后彻底解决的规定。我们希望这些规定将得到切实的履行。中美两国关系只有真正遵守互相尊重主权和领土完整、互不干涉内政的原则，才能继续取得健康的发展。

(据1982年9月5日《人民日报》)

生　词

(一)

1.	发表	(动) fābiǎo	issue
2.	声明	(名 动) shēngmíng	statement; state; declare
3.	统一	(动、名) tǒngyī	unite; reunification
4.	内政	(名) nèizhèng	internal affairs
5.	正常	(形) zhèngcháng	normal
6.	状态	(名) zhuàngtài	state
7.	事件	(名) shìjiàn	event
8.	众所周知	zhòng suǒ zhōuzhī	as all known; it is known to all

| 9. 关键 | (名) | guānjiàn | key; crux |
| 10. 至于 | (连) | zhìyú | as for; as to |

(二)

11. 阴影	(名)	yīnyǐng	shadow
12. 违反	(动)	wéifǎn	violate; run counter to
13. 武器	(名)	wǔqì	weapon
14. 实体	(名)	shítǐ	entity; substance
15. 对待	(动)	duìdài	treat
16. 主权	(名)	zhǔquán	sovereignty; sovereign right
17. 干涉	(动)	gānshè	interfere
18. 步骤	(名)	bùzhòu	step; move; measure
19. 彻底	(形)	chèdǐ	thorough; thoroughgoing
20. 履行	(动)	lǚxíng	carry out; fulfil
21. 尊重	(动)	zūnzhòng	respect
22. 领土	(名)	lǐngtǔ	territory
23. 完整	(形)	wánzhěng	integrity

问 题

1. 中国政府声明的主要精神是什么?
2. 什么问题曾经阻碍了中美关系正常化?
3. 这个问题彻底解决了没有?
4. 为什么说中美两国关系一直存在着阴影?
5. 中国政府对美国继续向台湾出售武器的立场是什么?
6. 中美两国关系怎样才能取得健康的发展?

第 四 课

一、范 句

1. 中 国 外交部 发言人 今天 发表 声明。
   Zhōngguó wàijiāobù fāyánrén jīntiān fābiǎo shēngmíng
   The Spokesman of the Ministry of Foreign Affairs of China issued a statement today.

2. 中国 政府 强烈 谴责 以色列 当局 野蛮
   Zhōngguó zhèngfǔ qiángliè qiǎnzé Yǐsèliè dāngjú yěmán
   屠杀 巴勒斯坦 平民。
   túshā Bālèsītǎn píngmín
   The Chinese Government strongly condemns the Israeli authorities for their savagely killing the Palestinian civilians.

3. 中 国 政府 强烈 谴责 以色列 当局 侵占
   Zhōngguó zhèngfǔ qiángliè qiǎnzé Yǐsèliè dāngjú qīnzhàn
   黎巴嫩 首都 贝鲁特 和 野蛮 屠杀 巴勒斯坦
   Líbānèn shǒudū Bèilǔtè hé yěmán túshā Bālèsītǎn
   平民 的 严重 罪行。
   píngmín de yánzhòng zuìxíng
   The Chinese Government strongly condemns the Israeli authorities for their grave crimes of invading and occupying Beirut, capital of Lebanon, and of savagely kil-

ling the Palestinian civilians.

1. 以色列 完全 蔑视 国际法 准则 和 有关
   Yǐsèliè wánquán mièshì guójìfǎ zhǔnzé hé yǒuguān
   各方 达成 的 协议。
   gèfāng dáchéng de xiéyì

   Israel totally despises the norms of international law and the agreement reached between the parties concerned.

5. 联合国 安理会 已 通过 决议, 要求 以色列
   Liánhéguó Ānlǐhuì yǐ tōngguò juéyì yāoqiú Yǐsèliè
   军队 立即 撤出 贝鲁特。
   jūnduì lìjí chèchū Bèilǔtè

   The United Nations Security Council has already adopted a resolution demanding that Israeli troops immediately withdraw from Beirut.

6. 决议 要求 以色列 军队 尊重 平民 的
   Juéyì yāoqiú Yǐsèliè jūnduì zūnzhòng píngmín de
   权利。
   quánlì

   The resolution demands that the Israeli troops respect the rights of civilians.

7. 以色列 当局 不仅 拒 不 执行 上述 协议,
   Yǐsèliè dāngjú bùjǐn jù bù zhíxíng shàngshù xiéyì
   而且 竟 对 巴勒斯坦 平民、 妇孺 进行
   érqiě jìng duì Bālèsītǎn píngmín fùrú jìnxíng
   屠杀。
   túshā

   The Israeli authorities not only refused to implement the above-mentioned resolution, but went so far as to massacre the innocent Palestinian civilians, including women and children,

8. 中国 政府 和 人民 坚决 支持 巴勒斯坦
   Zhōngguó zhèngfǔ hé rénmín jiānjué zhīchí Bālèsītǎn
   人民 的 正义 斗争。
   rénmín de zhèngyì dòuzhēng

   The Chinese Government and people firmly support the Palestinian people in the just struggle.

9. 中国 政府 和 人民 坚决 支持 黎巴嫩
   Zhōngguó zhèngfǔ hé rénmín jiānjué zhīchí Líbānèn
   政府 为 维护 主权 所 采取 的 措施。
   zhèngfǔ wèi wéihù zhǔquán suǒ cǎiqǔ de cuòshī

   The Chinese Government and people firmly support the measures the Lebanese Government has adopted for the maintenance of sovereignty.

10. 国际 社会 决 不 容许 以色列 当局 的
    Guójì shèhuì jué bù róngxǔ Yǐsèliè dāngjú de
    这种 暴行。
    zhèzhǒng bàoxíng

    The international community absolutely will not allow the Israeli authorities' atrocities.

11. 联合国 组织 应该 采取 有效 行动,
    Liánhéguó zǔzhī yīnggāi cǎiqǔ yǒuxiào xíngdòng
    制止 以色列 军队 的 暴行。
    zhìzhǐ Yǐsèliè jūnduì de bàoxíng

    The United Nations organizations should take prompt and effective actions to stop the Israeli troops' atrocities.

12. 一切 爱好 和平 和 主持 正义 的 国家
    Yīqiè àihào hépíng hé zhǔchí zhèngyì de guójiā
    和 人民 应该 采取 有效 的 行动, 迫使
    hé rénmín yīnggāi cǎiqǔ yǒuxiào de xíngdòng, pòshǐ
    以色列 侵略军 立即 无条件 地 撤出
    Yǐsèliè qīnlüèjūn lìjí wútiáojiàn de chèchū
    贝鲁特, 进而 全部 撤出 黎巴嫩。
    Bèilǔtè, jìnér quánbù chèchū Líbānèn.

    All the peace-loving and justice-upholding countries and peoples should take prompt and effective actions to force Israeli aggressor troops to withdraw immediately and unconditionally from Beirut and then from the whole Lebanon.

二、课 文

我国外交部发言人发表声明

强烈谴责以色列屠杀巴勒斯坦平民

新华社北京 9 月 19 日电 中国外交部发言人今天发表声明,强烈谴责以色列当局侵占黎巴嫩首都贝鲁特和野蛮屠杀巴勒斯坦平民的严重罪行。

声明说:"9 月 15 日,以色列完全蔑视国际法准则和有关各方达成的协议,悍然侵占贝鲁特西区。17 日,联合国安理会已通过决议要求以色列军队立即撤出贝鲁特

和尊重平民的权利。但是,以色列当局不仅蛮横地拒不执行上述协议,而且竟于18日对巴勒斯坦无辜平民、妇孺进行血腥屠杀。中国政府和人民强烈谴责以色列当局侵占黎巴嫩首都贝鲁特和野蛮屠杀巴勒斯坦平民的严重罪行。中国政府和人民坚决支持巴勒斯坦人民和阿拉伯各国人民的正义斗争,支持黎巴嫩政府为维护独立、主权和领土完整所采取的措施。"

声明说:"国际社会决不能容许以色列当局这种灭绝人性的暴行。联合国组织以及世界上一切爱好和平与主持正义的国家和人民应该立即采取有效行动,迅速制止以色列军队屠杀平民的暴行,迫使以色列侵略军立即、无条件地撤出贝鲁特,进而全部撤出黎巴嫩。"

(1982年)

三、生 词

1.	发言人	(名)	fāyánrén	spokesman
2.	强烈	(形)	qiángliè	strong
3.	谴责	(动)	qiǎnzé	condemn
4.	当局	(名)	dāngjú	the authorities
5.	侵占	(动)	qīnzhàn	invade
6.	野蛮	(形)	yěmán	barbarous; brutal; savage
7.	屠杀	(动)	túshā	kill
8.	罪行	(名)	zuìxíng	crime; guilt
9.	蔑视	(动)	mièshì	despise; defiance
10.	准则	(名)	zhǔnzé	norm

11.	悍然	(副)	hànrán	outrageously
12.	通过	(动)	tōngguò	adopt; pass
13.	决议	(名、动)	juéyì	resolution
14.	权利	(名)	quánlì	right
15.	蛮横	(形)	mánhèng	arrogantly; arbitrary
16.	执行	(动)	zhíxíng	implement
17.	上述		shàngshù	above-mentioned
18.	无辜	(形)	wúgū	innocent
19.	血腥	(形)	xuèxīng	bloody
20.	正义	(形、名)	zhèngyì	just
21.	维护	(动)	wéihù	maintain
22.	独立	(名)	dúlì	independence
23.	采取	(动)	cǎiqǔ	adopt
24.	措施	(名)	cuòshī	measure
25.	容许	(动)	róngxǔ	allow
26.	灭绝人性		mièjué rénxìng	inhuman; savage
27.	暴行	(名)	bàoxíng	atrocity; outrage
28.	爱好	(动、名)	àihào	love; like
29.	立即	(副)	lìjí	as soon as possible; at once
30.	制止	(动)	zhìzhǐ	stop
31.	迫使	(动)	pòshǐ	force
32.	无条件		wútiáojiàn	unconditionally
33.	进而	(连)	jìn'ér	then

专　名

1. 以色列　　Yǐsèliè　　　　Israel
2. 黎巴嫩　　Líbānèn　　　　Lebanon
3. 贝鲁特　　Bèilǔtè　　　　Beirut
4. 巴勒斯坦　Bālèsītǎn　　　Palestine
5. 联合国安理会
　　　　　　Liánhéguó Ānlǐhuì　the United Nations Security Council
6. 阿拉伯　　Ālābó　　　　　Arab

Translation

China Firmly Condemns Massacre of Palestinians

Beijing, September 19 (Xinhua) The spokesman of the Ministry of Foreign Affairs of the People's Republic of China issued a statement today, strongly condemning Israel for invading Beirut and savagely killing Palestinian civilians.

The statement says: "on 15 September Israel outrageously invaded and occupied west Beirut in total defiance of the norms of international law and the agreement reached between the parties concerned. On the 17th, the United Nations

Security Council adopted a resolution demanding that the Israeli troops immediately withdraw from Beirut and respect the rights of the civilians. However, the Israeli authorities not only arrogantly refused to implement the above-mentioned resolution, but on the 18th went so far as to massacre in cold blood the innocent Palestinian civilians, including women and children. The Chinese Government strongly condemns the Israeli authorities for their grave crimes of invading and occupying Beirut, capital of Lebanon, and of savagely killing the Palestinian civilians. The Chinese Government and people firmly support the Palestinian and other Arab peoples in their just struggles and support the measures the Lebanese Government has adopted for the maintenance of independence, sovereignty and territorial integrity."

The statement says: "the international community absolutely will not allow the Israeli authorities' inhuman atrocities. The United Nations Organizations and the peace-loving and justice-uphoding countries and peoples should take prompt and effective actions to stop as soon as possible the Israeli aggressor troops' atrocities of killing civilians and to force them to withdraw immediately and unconditionally from Beirut and then from the whole of Lebanon."

四、练　习

一、替换练习：

1. | 中国外交部发言人　　　　　 | 今天发表声明，强烈谴责以色
   | 中华人民共和国外交部 |
   | 中国政府 |

   列当局 | 侵占黎巴嫩首都贝鲁特 | 。
          | 野蛮屠杀巴勒斯坦平民 |
          | 大规模入侵黎巴嫩 |

2. 以色列当局完全 | 蔑视 | 国际法准则 |　　　，
                | 无视 | 国际社会的谴责 |
                | 违反 | 有关各方达成的协议 |

   悍然侵占贝鲁特西区。

3. 以色列当局对巴勒斯坦 | 无辜平民 | 进行了
                      | 妇女和儿童 |
                      | 难民 |

   | 血腥 | 屠杀。
   | 野蛮 |
   | 灭绝人性的 |

53

4．中国政府和人民坚决支持 | 巴勒斯坦人民 | 的正
　　　　　　　　　　　　　 | 阿拉伯各国人民 |
　　　　　　　　　　　　　 | 第三世界国家人民 |
　　　　　　　　　　　　　 | 非洲人民争取民族独立 |

义斗争。

5．联合国组织应该立即采取有效的措施，迫使以色列侵略军 | 停止屠杀巴勒斯坦平民的暴行 | 。
　　　　　　　　　　　　　　　　　　　　　　　　　　 | 无条件撤出贝鲁特 |
　　　　　　　　　　　　　　　　　　　　　　　　　　 | 全部撤出黎巴嫩 |

二、完成下列句子：

1．中国政府今天发表声明，……

2．以色列当局蔑视国际法准则，……

3．联合国安理会通过决议，要求……

4．中国政府和人民坚决支持……

5．世界上一切爱好和平的国家和人民应该立即行动起来，……

三、选词填空：

1．中国政府发表声明，_____谴责以色列当局侵略巴黎嫩。　（强烈、热烈）

2．以色列侵占黎巴嫩首都贝鲁特，违反了国际法准则和有关各方_____的协议。　（完成、达成）

3．9月17日，联合国安理会_____决议，要求以色列军队立即撤出贝鲁特。　（通过、经过）

4. 以色列当局不仅拒不_____联合国的有关决议，反而对巴勒斯坦无辜平民进行大屠杀。　（实行、执行）
5. 黎巴嫩政府为了_____国家独立、主权和领土完整采取了必要的措施。　（爱护、维护）
6. 一切爱好和平和主持正义的国家和人民应该立即行动起来，迅速_____以色列军队屠杀巴勒斯坦平民的暴行。
（停止、制止）

四、熟悉下列词组：

1.

强烈	谴责
	要求
	反对
	抗议

2.

侵占	别国领土
侵略	
侵入	

3.

维护	民族独立
	国家主权
	领土完整
	世界和平

4.

拒不执行	上述决议
	有关规定
	国际协定
	双方合同

5.

爱好和平的	国家
主持正义的	
社会主义	
资本主义	
第三世界	
不结盟	

6.

无条件（地）	撤军
	投降
	停火
	谈判
	遵守
	执行

五、阅 读

安理会举行紧急会议一致通过决议

谴责以色列野蛮屠杀巴勒斯坦人的罪行

据新华社联合国 9 月 19 日电 联合国安理会在今天凌晨举行的紧急会议上一致通过决议，谴责以色列野蛮屠杀巴勒斯坦人民的罪行，并决定把联合国派驻贝鲁特的观察员 10 人增加到 50 人。

决议要求联合国秘书长佩雷斯·德奎利亚尔立即同黎巴嫩政府磋商，商讨联合国可能采取的进一步措施，"其中包括有可能部署联合国部队，以帮助黎巴嫩政府确保对贝鲁特市及其周围的平民的保护"。决议还要求联合国秘书长在 48 小时之内就此向安理会作出报告。

在通过决议之前进行的辩论中，约旦和巴勒斯坦解放组织的代表谴责以色列军队在黎巴嫩基督教民兵的帮助下屠杀巴勒斯坦人。巴解观察员扎赫迪·特齐说："1500 名无辜平民被屠杀，大多数是妇女和孩子。男人被抓起来，背靠墙地排着，完全纳粹式地被枪杀。"

中国代表梁于藩在发言中说，"中国政府和人民再次最强烈地谴责以色列军队对贝鲁特西区的侵略和法西斯残暴行为。"他强调说，安理会应当考虑采取紧急和有效的措施，切实保证安理会520决议和有关决议的完全实施，以恢复贝鲁特正常的和平生活和黎巴嫩的主权,使巴勒斯坦和黎巴嫩的平民免遭进一步的屠杀和其它残暴行为。"

(1982 年)

生　词

1. 凌晨　　（名）língchén　　before dawn
2. 紧急　　（形）jǐnjí　　urgent
3. 观察员　（名）guāncháyuán　observer
4. 秘书长　（名）mìshūzhǎng　secretary-general
5. 磋商　　（动）cuōshāng　　consult
6. 部署　　（动）bùshǔ　　dispose; deploy
7. 部队　　（名）bùduì　　army
8. 确保　　（动）quèbǎo　　ensure; guarantee
9. 辩论　　（动）biànlùn　　argue; debate
10. 基督教　（名）Jīdūjiào　Christianity
11. 民兵　　（名）mínbīng　militia
12. 纳粹　　（名）Nàcuì　　Nazi
13. 考虑　　（动）kǎolǜ　　think over; consider
14. 实施　　（动）shíshī　　implement; put into effect
15. 恢复　　（动）huīfù　　recover; recapture

专　名

1. 佩雷斯·德奎利亚尔
　　　　　Pèiléisī·Dékuílìyà'ěr　人名
2. 约旦　　Yuēdàn　　Jordan

3. 扎赫迪·特齐　　Zhāhèdí·Tèqí　　　人名
4. 梁于藩　　　　Liáng Yúfān　　　　人名

问　题

1. 联合国安理会在什么时候举行了紧急会议？为什么？
2. 这次安理会紧急会议通过了什么决议？
3. 决议对联合国秘书长有哪些具体要求？
4. 通过决议之前，代表们作了什么事情？
5. 在会议辩论中，巴解观察员介绍了什么情况？
6. 中国代表在发言中表明的立场是什么？
7. 中国代表为什么强调安理会应采取紧急有效的措施？

第 五 课

一、范 句

1. 叶 剑 英 今天 发表 谈话， 进一步 阐明
   Yè Jiànyīng jīntiān fābiǎo tánhuà， jìnyībù chǎnmíng
   关于 台湾 回归 祖国， 实现 和平 统一
   guānyú Táiwān huíguī zǔguó， shíxiàn hépíng tǒngyī
   的 方 针 政策。
   de fāngzhēn zhèngcè
   Ye Jianying elaborated today on the policy concerning the return of Taiwan to the motherland for the realization of China's peaceful reunification.

2. 我 们 建 议 举行 中国 共产党 和
   Wǒmen jiànyì jǔxíng Zhōngguó Gòngchǎndǎng hé
   中国 国民党 两 党 对等 谈判。
   Zhōngguó Guómíndǎng liǎng dǎng duìděng tánpàn
   We propose that talks be held between the Communist Party of China and the Kuomintang of China on a reciprocal basis.

3. 海峡 两 岸 各 族 人民 迫切 希望 互通
   Hǎixiá liǎng àn gè zú rénmín pòqiè xīwàng hùtōng
   音 讯， 亲人 团聚。
   yīnxùn， qīnrén tuánjù

It is the urgent desire of the people of all nationalities on both sides of the straits to communicate with each other, reunite with their families and relatives.

4. 我们 建议 双方 共同 为 通邮、
   Wǒmen jiànyì shuāngfāng gòngtóng wèi tōngyóu
   通商、 通航 提供 方便， 达成 有关
   tōngshāng tōngháng tígōng fāngbiàn dáchéng yǒuguān
   协议。
   xiéyì

   We propose that the two sides make arrangements to facilitate the exchange of mails, trade, air and shipping services, and reach an agreement thereupon.

5. 国家 实现 统一 后， 中央 政府 不
   Guójiā shíxiàn tǒngyī huò zhōngyāng zhèngfǔ bù
   干预 台湾 地方 事务。
   gānyù Táiwān dìfāng shìwù

   After the country is reunified, the Central Government will not interfere with local affairs on Taiwan.

6. 台湾 现行 社会、 经济 制度 不 变，
   Táiwān xiànxíng shèhuì jīngjì zhìdù bù biàn
   生活 方式 不 变。
   shēnghuó fāngshì bù biàn

   Taiwan's current social-economic system will remain unchanged, so will its way of life.

7. 私人 财产、 房屋、 土地、 企业 所有权
   Sīrén cáichǎn fángwū tǔdì qǐyè suǒyǒuquán
   不 受 侵犯。
   bù shòu qīnfàn

There will be no encroachment on the proprietary rights over private property, houses, land and enterprises.

8. 台湾 当局 和 各 界 代表 人士 可 担任
　　Táiwān dāngjú hé gè jiè dàibiǎo rénshì kě dānrèn
　　全国性　　　政治　　机构　的　　领导　　职务。
　　quánguóxìng zhèngzhì jīgòu de lǐngdǎo zhíwù

People in authority and representative personages of various circles in Taiwan may take up posts of leadership in national political bodies.

9. 台湾 各 族 人民 愿 回 祖国 大陆 定居
　　Táiwān gè zú rénmín yuàn huí zǔguó dàlù dìngjū
　　者，　 保证　 妥善　 安排。
　　zhě bǎozhèng tuǒshàn ānpái

For the poeple of all nationalities in Taiwan who wish to come and settle on the mainland, it is guaranteed that proper arrangement will be made for them.

10. 欢迎　　　台湾　　工 商 界　　人士 回 祖国
　　Huānyíng Táiwān gōngshāngjiè rénshì huí zǔguó
　　大陆　 投资，兴办　各种　 经济　 事业。
　　dàlù tóuzī xīngbàn gèzhǒng jīngjì shìyè

Industrialists and businessmen in Taiwan are welcome to invest and engage in various economic undertakings on the mainland.

11. 统一 祖国，　人人 有 责。
　　Tǒngyī zǔguó rénrén yǒu zé

The reunification of the motherland is the resposibility of all Chinese.

12. 我们 热诚 欢迎 台湾 各 族 人民
    Wǒmen rèchéng huānyíng Táiwān gè zú rénmín
    通过 各种 渠道、采取 各种 方式
    tōngguò gèzhǒng qúdào cǎiqǔ gèzhǒng fāngshì
    提供 建议，共 商 国是。
    tígōng jiànyì gòng shāng guóshì

We sincerely welcome people of all nationalities in Taiwan to make proposals and suggestions regarding affairs of state through various channels and in various ways.

二、课 文

叶剑英委员长进一步阐明台湾回归祖国
实现和平统一的方针政策

建议举行两党对等谈判实行第三次合作

新华社北京 9 月 30 日电 全国人民代表大会常务委员会委员长叶剑英，今天向新华社记者发表谈话，进一步阐明关于台湾回归祖国，实现和平统一的方针政策：

（一）为了尽早结束中华民族陷于分裂的不幸局面，我们建议举行中国共产党和中国国民党两党对等谈判，实行第三次合作，共同完成祖国统一大业。双方可先派人接触，充分交换意见。

（二）海峡两岸各族人民迫切希望互通音讯、亲人团聚、开展贸易、增进了解。我们建议双方共同为通邮、通商、通航、探亲、旅游以及开展学术、文化、体育交流提供方便，达成有关协议。

（三）国家实现统一后，台湾可作为特别行政区，享有高度的自治权，并可保留军队。中央政府不干预台湾地方事务。

（四）台湾现行社会、经济制度不变，生活方式不变，同外国的经济、文化关系不变。私人财产、房屋、土地、企业所有权、合法继承权和外国投资不受侵犯。

（五）台湾当局和各界代表人士，可担任全国性政治机构的领导职务，参与国家管理。

（六）台湾地方财政遇有困难时，可由中央政府酌情补助。

（七）台湾各族人民、各界人士愿回祖国大陆定居者，保证妥善安排，不受歧视，来去自由。

（八）欢迎台湾工商界人士回祖国大陆投资，兴办各种经济事业，保证其合法权益和利润。

（九）统一祖国，人人有责。我们热诚欢迎台湾各族人民、各界人士、民众团体通过各种渠道、采取各种方式提供建议，共商国是。

(1981年)

三、生　词

1. 阐明　　（动）chǎnmíng　　expound; clarify;

			elaborate
2.	建议	(动、名) jiànyì	propose; suggest
3.	陷于	(动) xiànyú	fall into
4.	分裂	(动、名) fēnliè	split; separation
5.	不幸	(形) bùxìng	unfortunate
6.	大业	(名) dàyè	great cause
7.	接触	(动) jiēchù	meet with; come into contact with
8.	充分	(形) chōngfèn	full
9.	海峡	(名) hǎixiá	straits
10.	迫切	(形) pòqiè	urgent
11.	互通音讯	hùtōng yīnxùn	communicate with each orther
12.	亲人团聚	qīnrén tuánjù	reunite with one's families and relatives
13.	通邮	tōngyóu	accessible by postal communication; exchange of mails
14.	通商	tōngshāng	have trade relations
15.	通航	tōngháng	be open to navigation or air traffic
16.	旅游	(动、名) lǚyóu	tour
17.	学术	(名) xuéshù	learning; academic
18.	特别行政区	tèbié xíngzhèngqū	special administrative region
19.	享有	(动) xiǎngyǒu	enjoy

20.	自治权	（名）	zìzhìquán	autonomy
21.	保留	（动）	bǎoliú	retain; reserve
22.	军队	（名）	jūnduì	armed forces
23.	干预	（动）	gānyù	interfere with
24.	事务	（名）	shìwù	affairs
25.	社会	（名）	shèhuì	society
26.	制度	（名）	zhìdù	system
27.	生活方式		shēnghuó fāngshì	way of life
28.	私人	（形）	sīrén	personal; private
29.	财产	（名）	cáichǎn	property
30.	所有权	（名）	suǒyǒuquán	proprietary rights
31.	继承权	（名）	jìchéngquán	right of inheritance
32.	投资	（动、名）	tóuzī	invest; investment
33.	全国性	（形）	quánguóxìng	national; nation wide
34.	参与	（动）	cānyù	participate in
35.	管理	（动）	guǎnlǐ	manage; administer; run
36.	财政	（名）	cáizhèng	finance
37.	酌情		zhuóqíng	take into consideration the circumstance
38.	补助	（动、名）	bǔzhù	subsidize; sudsidy; allowance
39.	定居	（动）	dìngjū	settle down
40.	保证	（动）	bǎozhèng	guarantee; pledge
41.	安排	（动）	ānpái	arrange
42.	歧视	（动）	qíshì	discriminate against

43.	工商界	（名）	gōng-shāngjiè	industrial and commercial circles
44.	兴办	（动）	xīngbàn	initiate; set up; engage in
45.	权益	（名）	quányì	right and interest
46.	利润	（名）	lìrùn	profit
47.	责	（名）	zé	duty; responsibility
48.	热诚	（形）	rèchéng	warm and sincere; cordial
49.	民众团体		mínzhòng tuántǐ	mass organization
50.	渠道	（名）	qúdào	channel
51.	国是	（名）	guóshì	affairs of state

专　名

叶剑英　　　Yè Jiànyīng　　　人名

Translation

Chairman Ye Jianying's Elaborations on Policy Concerning Return of Taiwan To Motherland and Peaceful Reunification

Beijing, September 30 (Xinhua) Ye Jianying, Chairman of the Standing Committee of the National People's Congress, in an interview with a Xinhua correspondent today elaborated on the policy concerning the return of Taiwan to the motherland for the realization of China's peaceful reunification:

(1) In order to bring an end to the unfortunate separation of the Chinese nation as early as possible, we propose that talks be held between the Communist Party of China and the Kuomintang of China on a reciprocal basis so that the two parties will co-operate for the third time to accomplish the great cause of national reunification. The two sides may first send people to meet for an exhaustive exchange of views.

(2) It is the urgent desire of the people of all nationalities on both sides of the straits to communicate with each other, reunite with their families and relatives, develop trade and increase mutual understanding. We propose that the two sides make arrangements to facilitate the exchange of mails, trade, air and shipping services, family reunions and visits by relatives and tourists as well as academic, cultural and sports exchanges, and reach an agreement thereupon.

(3) After the country is reunified, Taiwan can enjoy a high degree of autonomy as a special administrative region and it can retain its armed forces. The Central Government will not interfere with local affairs on Taiwan.

(4) Taiwan's current social-economic system will remain unchanged, so will its way of life and its economic and cultural relations with foreign countries. There will be no encroachment on the proprietary rights and lawful right of

inheritance over private property, houses, land and enterprises, or on foreign investments.

(5) People in authority and representative personages of various circles in Taiwan may take up posts of leadership in national political bodies and participate in running the state.

(6) When Taiwan's local finance is in difficulty, the Central Government may subsidize it as is fit for the circumstances.

(7) For people of all nationalities and public figures of various circles in Taiwan who wish to come and settle on the mainland, it is guaranteed that proper arrangements will be made for them, that there will be no discrimination against them, and that they will have the freedom of entry and exit.

(8) Industrialists and businessmen in Taiwan are welcome to invest and engage in various economic undertakings on the mainland, and their legal rights, interests and profits are guaranteed.

(9) The reunification of the motherland is the responsibility of all Chinese. We sincerely welcome people of all nationalities, public figures of all circles and all mass organizations in Taiwan to make proposals and suggestions regarding affairs of state through various channels and in various ways.

四、练 习

一、替换练习：

1. 叶剑英今天向新华社记者发表谈话，进一步 | 阐明 / 阐述 / 说明 |

   关于台湾回归祖国，实现和平统一的方针政策。

2. 叶剑英建议 | 举行两党对等谈判，实行第三次合作。/ 双方先派人接触，充分交换意见。|

3. 建议双方共同为 | 通邮、通商、通航 / 探亲、旅游 / 开展学术、文化、体育交流 | 提供方便，达成有关协议。

4. 国家实现统一后，台湾 | 现行社会经济制度 / 生活方式 / 同外国的经济文化联系 | 不变。

5. 欢迎台湾各界人士回祖国大陆 | 定居 / 投资 |，保证

   | 妥善安排，来去自由 / 其合法权益和利润 |。

6. 我们热诚欢迎台湾 [各族人民／各界人士／民众团体] 通过各种渠道，采取各种方式提供建议，共商 [国是／国事／国家大事]。

二、把下列词语分别填入各句：

　　充分　妥善　现行　尽早　共同　迫切　合法　高度

1. 为了 _____ 结束中华民族的分裂局面，我们建议国民党和共产党举行对等谈判。
2. 当前，台湾海峡两岸人民 _____ 希望互通音讯，亲人团聚，开展贸易。
3. 双方可先派人接触，_____ 交换意见。
4. 国家实现统一后，台湾享有 _____ 的自治权。
5. 欢迎台湾工商界人士回祖国大陆兴办各种经济事业，保证其 _____ 权益。
6. 回到祖国大陆定居的人，保证 _____ 安排，不受歧视，来去自由。
7. 国家实现统一后，台湾 _____ 社会经济制度不变。
8. 中国共产党希望，国共两党实行第三次合作，_____ 完成祖国统一大业。

三、选词填空：

1. 叶剑英委员长今天向新华社记者 _____ 谈话，进一步阐明台湾回归祖国，实现和平统一的方针政策。

　　　　　　　　　　　　　　　　　　（发表、公布）

2．叶剑英建议举行中国共产党和国民党两党_____谈判。
　　　　　　　　　　　　　　　　　　（平等、对等）
3．海峡两岸各族人民希望开展学术文化_____。
　　　　　　　　　　　　　　　　　　（交换、交流）
4．两党可先派人接触，充分_____意见。
　　　　　　　　　　　　　　　　　　（交换、交流）
5．国家　　　和平统一后，台湾可成为特别行政区。
　　　　　　　　　　　　　　　　　　（实现、实行）
6．中国共产党建议，国共两党_____第三次合作。
　　　　　　　　　　　　　　　　　　（实现、实行）
7．台湾当局和各界代表人士可担任全国性政治机构的领导职务，_____国家管理。　　（干预、参与）
8．台湾现行社会经济制度不受，私人财产、企业所有权、合法继承权和外国投资不受_____。（侵略、侵犯）

四、熟悉下列词组：

1.

阐明	方针政策
	观点
	中国政府的立场

2.

互通	音讯
	音信
	消息
	情报
	有无

3.

提供	方便
	便利
	机会
	建议

4.

参与	国家管理
	制订计划
	会议准备工作
	其事

5.	酌情	补助
		处理
		解决
		安排

6.	不受	侵犯
		歧视
		影响

五、阅　读

叶委员长提出的九条方针政策大得人心
一年来在台湾岛和海内外影响与日俱增

新华社北京9月29日电　新华社记者报道：叶剑英委员长去年国庆前夕提出的关于台湾回归祖国、实现和平统一的九条方针政策，一年来在台湾岛和海内外产生了深刻的影响，这种影响正在与日俱增。

尽管台湾人民对祖国大陆的声音还处于被隔绝的状态，他们还是知道了"九条"的内容，并且广为传播。台湾各阶层同胞强烈要求和谈、统一、与亲人团聚的声浪，正有力地冲击着台湾当局"不接触、不谈判、不妥协"的堤防。

一年来，从到大陆、到海外的台湾同胞的谈论中，从无数来自台湾的家书中，从台湾和海外一些华人报刊的报道中，都透露出台湾同胞对"九条"的赞赏和支持。

许多台湾同胞认为，九条方针政策是宽厚的、**具体的**，照顾到了台湾各方面的利益，共产党和平解决台湾问题具有诚意。有的说，"听了中共宣布的这九条，就象吃了一颗定心丸。"

散居在台湾各地的大陆籍老人，经常和老乡聚在一起，互相叮咛要保重身体，以便在有生之年回故乡同亲人团聚。他们的后代和从没有到过大陆的台湾籍同胞，都渴望了解祖国大陆的真实情况。收听大陆广播的人越来越多了。今年，海外拍摄的介绍大陆锦绣河山及人民生活的电影电视，曾一度在台湾放映，在台湾同胞当中引起强烈的兴趣。许多人看了《万里长城》等影片后，纷纷要求重播，台湾当局随即下令停止播放。

在国民党上层也并不都是坚持"不接触、不谈判、不妥协"立场的。其中有的是"立法委员"、"国策顾问"，有的是宣传部门的负责人，等等，或公开表示"国共和谈不失为国家统一之手段"，"不妨一试"；或认为"统一问题已经面临了一个必须突破、也可能突破的关键时刻"，应该"准备中国的问题必须在八十年代内加以解决"。

（1982 年）

生　词

1. 海内外　　　　hǎinèi-wài　　all the world
2. 与日俱增　　　yǔ rì jù zēng　grow with each passing day
3. 隔绝　　（动）géjué　　　　completely cut off; isolated

4.	冲击	（动）	chōngjī	lash; pound
5.	妥协	（动）	tuǒxié	compromise
6.	堤防	（名）	dīfáng	dyke; embankment
7.	宽厚	（形）	kuānhòu	generous
8.	定心丸	（名）	dìngxīnwán	sth. capable of setting sb.'s mind at ease
9.	叮咛	（动）	dīngníng	warn; urge again and again
10.	渴望	（动）	kěwàng	thirst for; long for
11.	拍摄	（动）	pāishè	take (a picture); shoot
12.	锦绣山河		jǐnxiù shānhé	a beautiful land
13.	放映	（动）	fàngyìng	show; project
14.	宣传	（名、动）	xuānchuán	propagate
15.	不失为		bùshīwéi	can yet be regarded as
16.	不妨	（副）	bùfāng	might as well
17.	面临	（动）	miànlín	be faced with
18.	突破	（动）	tūpò	break through

问 题

1. 叶剑英委员长提出的关于台湾回归祖国、实现和平统一的九条方针政策产生了什么影响？
2. 台湾同胞对"九条"方针态度如何？
3. 为什么有人说，听了中共宣布的"九条"，就象吃了一颗定心丸？
4. 在台湾的大陆籍老人对"九条"有什么反应？
5. 台湾同胞关心祖国大陆的情况吗？
6. 台湾当局对"九条"采取了什么立场？
7. 国民党上层人士都赞成台湾当局的立场吗？

第 六 课

一、范 句

1. 第五 届 全国 人民 代表 大会 第五 次
   Dì-wǔ Jiè Quánguó Rénmín Dàibiǎo Dàhuì dì-wǔ cì
   会议 今天 下午 在 人民 大会堂 开幕。
   huìyì Jīntiān xiàwǔ zài Rénmín Dàhuìtáng kāimù
   The 5th Session of the 5th National People's Congress (NPC) opened in the Great Hall of the People this afternoon.

2. 彭 真 代表 宪法 修改 委员会 在 会上
   Péng Zhēn dàibiǎo Xiànfǎ Xiūgǎi Wěiyuánhuì zài huìshang
   作了 关于 宪法 修改 草案 的 报告。
   zuòle guānyú xiànfǎ xiūgǎi cǎo'àn de bàogào
   Peng Zhen delivered a report on the draft of the revised Constitution on behalf of the Committee for the Revision of the Constitution on the meeting.

3. 现行 宪法 是 1978 年 3 月 五 届 人大
   Xiànxíng xiànfǎ shi yījiǔqībā nián sānyuè Wǔ Jiè Réndà
   第一 次 会议 上 通过 的。
   dìyī cì huìyì shang tōngguò de
   The Constitution currently in force was adopted by the NPC at its first session in March 1978.

4. 现行宪法在许多方面已经同现实情况不相符合，同国家生活的需要不相适应，有必要对它进行全面的修改。
   Xiànxíng xiànfǎ zài xǔduō fāngmiàn yǐjing tóng xiànshí qíngkuàng bù xiāng fúhé, tóng guójiā shēnghuó de xūyào bù xiāng shìyìng, yǒu bìyào duì ta jìnxíng quánmiàn de xiūgǎi.

   The Constitution as it stands does not conform in many respects to present realities, nor does it suit the needs of the life of the state, thus, an all-round revision is necessary.

5. 全民讨论的规模之大、参加人数之多、影响之广，足以表明全国工人、农民、知识分子和其他各界人士管理国家事务的政治热情的高涨。
   Quánmín tǎolùn de guīmó zhī dà, cānjiā rénshù zhī duō, yǐngxiǎng zhī guǎng, zúyǐ biǎomíng quánguó gōngrén, nóngmín, zhīshifènzǐ hé qítā gèjiè rénshì guǎnlǐ guójiā shìwù de zhèngzhì rèqíng de gāozhǎng.

   The unprecedented scale of the discussion of the whole people, the large number of people participating in the discussions and the far-reaching influence so engendered all demonstrate the soaring political enthusiasm of the workers, peasants, intellectuals and people from other circles in managing state affairs.

6. 通过 全 民 讨论，发扬 民主， 使 宪法 的
   Tōngguò quán mín tǎolùn fāyáng mínzhǔ shǐ xiànfǎ de
   修改 更 好 地 集中了 群众 的 智慧。
   xiūgǎi gèng hǎo de jízhōngle qúnzhòng de zhìhuì。

   The discussion of revised Constitution by all the people gave scope to democracy, thereby pooling the wisdom of the people.

7. 宪法 修改 草案 的 总 的 指导 思想 是
   Xiànfǎ xiūgǎi cǎo'àn de zǒng de zhǐdǎo sīxiǎng shi
   四 项 基本 原则。
   sì xiàng jīběn yuánzé

   The four cardinal principles constituted the overall guidelines for drafting the revised Constitution.

8. 四 项 基本 原则 是 全国 各 族 人民
   Sì xiàng jīběn yuánzé shi quánguó gè zú rénmín
   团结 前进 的 共同 的 政治 基础， 也
   tuánjié qiánjìn de gòngtóng de zhèngzhì jīchǔ, yě
   是 社会主义 现代化 建设 顺利 进行 的
   shì shèhuìzhǔyì xiàndàihuà jiànshè shùnlì jìnxíng de
   根本 保证。
   gēnběn bǎozhèng

   The four cardinal principles form the common political basis for the united advance of the people of all nationalities in our country and are the basic guarantee for the smooth progress of our socialist modernization.

9. 这个 宪法 修改 草案 继承 和 发展了
   Zhège xiànfǎ xiūgǎi cǎo'àn jìchéng hé fāzhǎnle
   1954 年 宪法 的 基本 原则。
   yījiǔwǔsì nián xiànfǎ de jīběn yuánzé

The draft of revised Constitution has carried forward and developed the basic principles of the 1954 Constitution.

10. 它 充分 注意 总结 我 国 社会主义 发展
    Tā chōngfèn zhùyì zǒngjié wǒ guó shèhuìzhǔyì fāzhǎn
    的 丰富 经验， 也 注意 吸取 国际 的
    de fēngfù jīngyàn, yě zhùyì xīqǔ guójì de
    经验。
    jīngyàn

    It incorporates a careful summary of the rich experience of China's socialist development and drawing on international experience.

11. 它 既 考虑 到 当前 的 现实， 又 考虑
    Tā jì kǎolù dào dāngqián de xiànshí, yòu kǎolù
    到 发展 的 前景。
    dào fāzhǎn de qiánjǐng

    It also takes into account both the current situation and the prospects for development.

12. 这 是 一 部 有 中国 特色 的、 适应
    Zhè shì yī bù yǒu Zhōngguó tèsè de, shìyìng
    新 的 历史 时期 社会主义 现代化 建设
    xīn de lìshǐ shíqī shèhuìzhǔyì xiàndàihuà jiànshè
    需要 的 长期 稳定 的 新 宪法。
    xūyào de chángqī wěndìng de xīn xiànfǎ

    The new Constitution is distinctively Chinese, suits the needs of China's socialist modernization in the new historical period and will remain valid for a considerable period of time.

二、课　文

五届人大五次会议在京开幕
彭真作关于宪法修改草案的报告

新华社北京11月26日电　第五届全国人民代表大会第五次会议今天下午在人民大会堂开幕。

宪法修改委员会副主任委员彭真代表宪法修改委员会，在会上作了关于宪法修改草案的报告。

彭真说，现行宪法是1978年3月第五届全国人民代表大会第一次会议通过的。中国共产党十一届三中全会以后，国家的政治生活、经济生活和文化生活发生了巨大的变化。现行宪法在许多方面已经同现实情况不相符合，同国家生活的需要不相适应，有必要对它进行全面的修改。

彭真指出，这次宪法的修改、讨论工作前后进行了两年之久，是做得相当认真、慎重和周到的。全民讨论的规模之大、参加人数之多、影响之广，足以表明全国工人、农民、知识分子和其他各界人士管理国家事务的政治热情的高涨。通过全民讨论，发扬民主，使宪法的修改更好地集中了群众的智慧。

彭真说，宪法修改草案的总的指导思想是四项基本原则。这是全国各族人民团结前进的共同的政治基础，也是社会主义现代化建设顺利进行的根本保证。

他说，这个宪法修改草案继承和发展了1954年宪法的基本原则，充分注意总结我国社会主义发展的丰富经验，也注意吸取国际的经验；既考虑到当前的现实，又考虑到发展的前景。这是一部有中国特色的、适应新的历史时期社会主义现代化建设需要的、长期稳定的新宪法。

（1982 年）

三、生　词

1. 开幕　　　（动）kāimù　　　open
2. 宪法　　　（名）xiànfǎ　　　constitution
3. 草案　　　（名）cǎo'àn　　　draft
4. 现行　　　　　 xiànxíng　　 currently in effect; in force
5. 现实　　　（形）xiànshí　　　realistic
6. 适应　　　（动）shìyìng　　　suit; fit
7. 慎重　　　（形）shènzhòng　　careful
8. 周到　　　（形）zhōudào　　　thoughtful; attentive and satisfactory
9. 知识分子　（名）zhīshi fènzǐ　intellectual
10. 高涨　　　（动）gāozhǎng　　soar; rise; upsurge
11. 智慧　　　（名）zhìhuì　　　wisdom
12. 四项基本原则
　　　　　　　　sìxiàng jīběn yuánzé　four cardinal principles (adherence to the socialist

road, the peoples democratic dictatorship, the leadership of the Communist Party of China and Marxism-Leninism and Mao Zedong Thought)

13. 继承　　（动）jìchéng　　inherit; carry on
14. 吸取　　（动）xīqǔ　　draw; absorb
15. 特色　　（名）tèsè　　characteristic; distinguishing feature

专　名

1. 彭真　　　　　　Péng Zhēn　　人名
2. 宪法修改委员会　Xiànfǎ Xiūgǎi Wěiyuánhuì
　　　　　　　　　Committee for the Revision of the Constitution

Translation

Peng Zhen Delivered a Report on the Draft of the Revised Constitution

Beijing November 26 (Xinhua) The 5th Session of the

5th National People's Congress (NPC) of the People's Republic of China opened in the Great Hall of the People this afternoon.

Peng Zhen, Vice-Chairman of the Committee for the Revision of the Costitution, delivered a report on the draft of the revised Constitution on behalf of the committee on the meeting.

He said that the Constitution currently in force was adopted by the 5th NPC at its first session in March 1978. Since the Third Plenary Session of the 11th Party Central Committee held at the end of 1978, tremendous changes have taken place in the country's political, economic and cultural life. The Constitution as it stands does not conform in many respects to present realities, nor does it suit the needs of the life of the state. Thus, an all-round revision is necessary.

Peng Zhen said that two years had been spent discussing and revising the Constitution conscientiously, carefully and meticulously. The unprecedented scale of the discussion of the revised Constitution, the large number of people participating in the discussions and the far-reaching influence so engendered all demonstrate the soaring political enthusiasm of the workers, peasants, intellectuals and people from other circles in managing state affairs.

The discussions gave scope to democracy, thereby pooling the wisdom of the people.

The four cardinal principles—adherence to the socialist road, the people's democratic dictatorship, the leadership of the Communist Party of China, and Marxism-Leninism and

Mao Zedong Thought—constituted the overall guidelines for drafting the revised Constitution. These cardinal principles form the common political basis for the united advance of the people of all nationalities in our country and are the basic guarantee for the smooth progress of our socialist modernization, Peng Zhen said.

He pointed out that the present draft has carried forward and developed the basic principles of the 1954 Constitution while incorporating a careful summary of the rich experience of China's socialist development and drawing on international experience. It also takes into account both the current situation and the prospects for development. It is distinctively Chinese, suits the needs of China's socialist modernization in the new historical period and will remain valid for a considerable period of time.

四、练 习

一、替换练习：

1. | 彭真 / 赵紫阳 | 代表 | 宪法修改委员会 / 国务院 | 在会上作了关于 | 宪法修改草案 / 第六个五年计划 | 的报告。

2. 1978 年的宪法在许多方面同 | 现实情况 / 国家生活的需要 | 不相

符合 / 适应 。

3. 参加修改宪法讨论的 规模/人数/影响 之 大/多/广 ，足以表明全国人民政治热情的高涨。

4. 四项基本原则是 宪法修改草案 / 全国各族人民团结前进 / 我国四化建设 的 指导思想 / 共同政治基础 / 根本保证 。

二、选词填空：

1. 十一届三中全会以后，中国的情况发生了巨大的＿＿＿＿。
（变化　改变）

2. 在现代化建设中，必须＿＿＿＿轻视知识分子作用的思想。
（变化　改变）

3. 在宪法修改草案讨论过程中，各地充分＿＿＿＿民主，使宪法的修改更好地集中了广大群众的智慧。
（发展　发扬）

4. 1982年通过的宪法继承了1954年宪法的基本原则，并且有所＿＿＿＿。
（发展　发扬）

5. 由于各方面情况的变化，原来的宪法已经不适应当前国家生活的_____。 （必要　需要）
6. 四项基本原则是我们建国以来基本经验的总结，完全有_____写进宪法修改草案。 （必要　需要）
7. 原来的宪法在许多方面同现实情况不相符，所以这次进行了_____修改。 （总的　全面的）
8. 这次修改宪法_____要求是制定出一部具有中国特色的、适应新的历史时期需要的、长期稳定的新宪法。

（总的　全面的）

三、用指定的词语改写下列句子：
1. 1982年12月第五届全国人民代表大会第五次会议通过了中华人民共和国第四部宪法 （是……的）
2. 中国共产党十一届三中全会以后，国家的政治、经济、文化生活发生了很大的变化。 （自……以来）
3. 1978年的宪法在许多方面不适应国家生活的需要。

（同……不相适应）
4. 这个宪法修改草案在考虑到当前现实的同时，也考虑到今后发展的前景。 （既……又……）

四、熟悉下列词组：

1.
修改	宪法
	法律
	条约
	规定
	文章

2.
（会议）通过	宪法
	提案
	议案
	决议
	决定

| 3. | 现行 | 宪法
政策
制度
规定
办法 |

| 4. | 符合 | 需要
实际
要求
条件 |

| 5. | 适应 | 需要
情况
要求
潮流 |

| 6. | 发扬 | 民主
优点
优良传统
革命精神
共产主义风格 |

五、阅　读

五届全国人大五次会议举行全体大会
中华人民共和国第四部宪法庄严诞生

新华社北京12月4日电　中华人民共和国的第四部宪法今天庄严诞生。在第五届全国人民代表大会第五次会议今天下午举行的全体会议上，当大会执行主席习仲勋宣布大会以无记名投票方式通过了这部治国安邦的根本大法时，灯火辉煌的人民大会堂会场里，响起了雷鸣般的掌声。

五届全国人大有3,421位代表，出席今天大会的代表3,040人。少数民族代表穿上了民族服装，人们喜气洋洋，兴高采烈，大会堂里洋溢着欢乐的气氛。

　　大会先通过了本次会议通过宪法和各项议案的办法。办法规定，通过宪法采用无记名投票表决的方式，以全体代表的三分之二以上的多数通过；通过其他各项议案，采用举手表决方式，以全体代表的过半数通过。

　　会上宣读了中华人民共和国宪法修改草案全文。宪法修改草案除序言外共分四章、一百三十八条。大会接着通过了62名监票人名单；计票工作人员核对了出席今天大会的代表人数；监票人验了票箱。下午5时开始，代表们在大会堂内的30个票箱分别投下庄严的一票。大会还为年迈体弱的代表设立了一个流动票箱。叶剑英、谭震林等代表在流动票箱投了票。

　　投票完毕后监票人开箱清点票数。据总监票人报告，清点结果，发票3,040张，投票3,040张，投票与发票的数目相符，本次投票有效。

　　下午5时45分，习仲勋宣布：根据总监票人报告，有效票3,040张，其中同意票3,037张，反对票没有，**弃**权票3张。现在宣布：中华人民共和国宪法已由本次会议通过。这时，会场里响起热烈的掌声。

（1982年）

生　词

1. 庄严　　　（形）zhuānuyán　　solemn; dignified

2.	诞生	（动）	dànshēng	be born; come into being
3.	执行主席		zhíxíng zhǔxí	executive chairman
4.	无记名投票		wújìmíng tóupiào	secret ballot
5.	喜气洋洋		xǐqì yángyáng	full of joy; jubilantly
6.	灯火辉煌		dēnghuǒ huīhuáng	brilliantly illuminated
7.	雷鸣		léimíng	thunderous; thundery
8.	洋溢	（动）	yángyì	be permeated with; brim with
9.	气氛	（名）	qìfēn	atmosphere
10.	议案	（名）	yì'àn	proposal; motion
11.	表决	（动）	biǎojué	vote; decide by vote
12.	序言	（名）	xùyán	preface; foreword
13.	监票人	（名）	jiānpiàorén	scrutineer
14.	核对	（动）	héduì	check
15.	弃权		qìquán	abstain from voting

专　名

1.	习仲勋	Xí Zhòngxūn	人名
2.	谭震林	Tán Zhènlín	人名

问　题

1. 中国的宪法是由什么会议表决通过的？
2. 大会采用什么方式通过宪法？
3. 表决其他议案时，也需要采用同样的方式吗？
4. 请介绍一下大会投票的情况。
5. 投票的结果如何？
6. 大会通过的宪法是中华人民共和国的第几部宪法？有多少章？多少条？

第 七 课

一、范 句

1. 何　东　昌　要求　采取　积极　措施，努力　把
   Hé Dōngchāng yāoqiú cǎiqǔ jījí cuòshī nǔlì bǎ
   人力　资源　转化为　人才　资源。
   rénlì zīyuán zhuǎnhuàwéi réncái zīyuán

   He Dongchang has urged energetic efforts to transform resources of manpower into professionally competent labour.

2. 轻视　教育　和　科学　的　落后　思想　应
   Qīngshì jiàoyù hé kēxué de luòhòu sīxiǎng yīng
   逐步　得到　克服。
   zhúbù dédào kèfú

   The backward notion of looking down on education and science should be overcome step by step.

3. 目前　中国　教育　事业　的　内部　结构、
   Mùqián Zhōngguó jiàoyù shìyè de nèibù jiégòu
   制度和　管理　体制，已经　不　能　适应　形势
   zhìdù hé guǎnlǐ tǐzhì yǐjing bù néng shìyìng xíngshì
   发展　的　需要。
   fāzhǎn de xūyào

   The present structure and system of management of

Chinese education are no longer capable of keeping up with the changing situation.

4. 他 说， 对 外国 经验 一 定 要 取 分析
   Tā shuō duì wàiguó jīngyàn yīdìng yào qǔ fēnxī
   态度， 重大 改革 一 定 要 经过 试点，
   tàidù zhòngdà gǎigé yīdìng yào jīngguò shìdiǎn
   分 步骤 进行。
   fēn bùzhòu jìnxíng

   He said, in borrowing from foriegn experience, we must have an analytical attitude, and experiments must be carried out before any major steps for reform are adopted.

5. 何 东 昌 说， 必须 从 基础 教育 抓起，
   Hé Dōngchāng shuō bìxū cóng jīchǔ jiàoyù zhuāqǐ
   一 九 九 〇 年 前 在 全国 基本 普及
   yījiǔjiǔlíng nián qián zài quánguó jīběn pǔjí
   小学 教育。
   xiǎoxué jiàoyù

   He Dongchang said, it must emphasize on basic education aimed at achieving nation wide universal primary education by 1990.

6. 农 村 教育 必须 适应 农村 的 特点。
   Nóngcūn jiàoyù bìxū shìyìng nóngcūn de tèdiǎn
   Rural education must fit the rural special condition.

7. 教育 工作 近 几 年 已 呈现出
   Jiàoyù gōngzuò jìn jǐ nián yǐ chéngxiànchu

繁荣　　景象。
fánróng　jǐngxiàng

Bright prospects have emerged in education in recent years.

8. 中国　已　有　六百　多　个　县　基本　普及
Zhōngguó yǐ yǒu liùbǎi duō gè xiàn jīběn pǔjí-

了　小学　教育。
le xiǎoxué jiàoyù

More than 600 Chinese counties have in the main achieved universal primary school education.

9. 盲目　发展　普通　高中　的　做法　已经
Mángmù fāzhǎn pǔtōng gāozhōng de zuòfǎ yǐjing

扭　转。
niǔzhuǎn

The blind development of general high schools has been stopped.

10. 一九七八　年　恢复　招收　研究生　以来，
Yījiǔqībā nián huīfù zhāoshóu yánjiūshēng yǐlái

共　招收　研究生　四万　三千　多　人。
gòng zhāoshōu yánjiūsēhng sìwān sānqiān duō rén

Some 43000 post-graduates were enrolled since that system was revived in 1978.

11. 近　几　年，　向　国外　派出　了　一万　二千多
Jìn jǐ nián xiàng guówài pàichū le yīwān èrqiān duō

名　留学　人员。
míng liúxué rényuán

Some 12,000 students were sent abroad for advanced study in recent years.

12. 除了　国家　办　学　外，　许多　工厂、　民主
    Chúle guójiā bàn xué wài xǔduō gōngchǎng mínzhǔ
    党派、　社　会　团体　都　在　办学。
    dǎngpài shè huì tuántǐ dōu zài bànxué

Apart from state universities, many factories, democratic parties and mass organizations are opening schools on their own.

二、课　文

何东昌谈中国教育前景

新华社北京10月3日电　教育部长何东昌要求采取积极措施努力把人力资源转化为丰富的人才资源。他说，"教育是国家富强的基本条件之一"，党的十二大对教育的强调，必须成为人所共知的常识，让那种轻视教育和科学的落后思想逐步得到克服。

这位部长在今天《人民日报》上发表的文章中说，目前中国教育事业的内部结构、制度和管理体制等许多方面已经不能适应形势发展的需要，必须进行调整、改革。他说，三十多年以来的经验说明，"对外国经验一定要取分析态度，重大改革一定要经过试点，分步骤进行。"

在谈到教育改革时，何东昌提出了下列规划：必须从基础教育抓起，一九九〇年前在全国基本普及小学教育；加强中等职业技术教育，进一步改革中等教育的结

构；高等教育的概念要适当放宽，学制要实行多层次，办学形式要多样化；进一步发展电视、广播、函授教育，为提高干部、职工、教师和农民的文化科学水平服务；农村教育必须适应农村特点，要考虑农业、社队企业、农村建筑、商业、管理、卫生、师范等等方面人材的需要。

何东昌指出，教育工作近几年已呈现出繁荣景象。据二十五个省、市、自治区的不完全统计，已经有六百多个县（市、区）基本普及了小学教育；约占全国总数的百分之二十七。还有一大批公社和大队也已基本普及小学教育。盲目发展普通高中的作法已经扭转。一九八一年，专业学校在校学生的总数，约占整个高级中等教育阶段在校学生总数的百分之二十三点八，而一九七九年只占百分之十。

从一九七六年到一九八一年，全日制普通高等学校在校学生从五十六万五千人增加到一百二十八万人，翻了一番。一九七八年恢复招收研究生以来，五年共招收研究生四万三千多人，相当于一九四九年到一九六六年总数的一点七倍。几年来，向国外派出了各类留学人员共一万二千多人，接受了外国来华留学生四千多人。中国现在有近一千万人的教师队伍。除了国家办学外，许多工矿企业、民主党派、社会团体都在纷纷办学。

（1982年）

三、生　词

1. 教育　　　（名）jiàoyù　　　education
2. 资源　　　（名）zīyuán　　　resource
3. 转化　　　（动）zhuǎnhuà　　transform; change
4. 人才　　　（名）réncái　　　a person of ability; a talented person
5. 常识　　　（名）chángshí　　general knowledge; common sense
6. 落后　　　（形）luòhòu　　　backward; fall behind
7. 结构　　　（名）jiégòu　　　structure
8. 分析　　　（动）fēnxī　　　analyse
9. 态度　　　（名）tàidù　　　attitude
10. 试点　　　（动）shìdiǎn　　make experience; experimental unit
11. 下列　　　　　　 xiàliè　　listed below; following
12. 规划　　　（名）guīhuà　　 plan; programme
13. 概念　　　（名）gàiniàn　　concept; notion; idea
14. 学制　　　（名）xuézhì　　 educational system
15. 层次　　　（名）céngcì　　 administrative levels
16. 函授　　　（名）hánshòu　　teach by correspondence
17. 师范　　　（名）shīfàn　　 teacher-training; norm school
18. 呈现　　　（动）chéngxiàn　appear
19. 盲目　　　（形）mángmù　　 blind
20. 扭转　　　（动）niǔzhuǎn　 turn round; turn back
21. 翻一番　　　　 fānyīfān　 double

22. 招收　　（动）zhāoshōu　　recruit; take in

专　　名

何东昌　　Hé Dōngchāng　　人名

Translation

He Dongchang Outlines Prospects for China's Education

Beijing, October 3 (Xinhua) - Chinese Minister of Education He Dongchang has urged energetic efforts to transform China's rich resources of manpower into professionally competent labour. He called education "a prerequisite for China's development." The emphasis on education given by the Party's 12th Congress must be made known to all in the ountry so that the backward notion of looking down on education and science can be overcome step by step, he said.

Writing in today's "People's Daily", the minister said, the present structure and system of management of Chinese education were no longer capable of keeping up with the changing situation and so there must be readjustment and reform. He added, "in borrowing from foreign experience we must have an analytical attitude, and experiments must be carried out before any major steps for reform are adopted. This is also what we've learned from our past three decades of experience".

For reform of education, He Dongchang outlined the following programme: emphasis on basic education aimed at achieving nationwide universal primary education by 1990; restructuring secondary education by increasing vocational training; a broader concept of higher education with varied curriculum and forms of schooling reaching different levels, and developing TV, radio, correspondence education for cadres, workers, teachers and peasants. Rural education must fit the rural development programs, including the urgent need for agronomists, commune enterprise managers, architects, economists, health workers and teachers.

He Dongchang listed the following figures to support his conclusion that efforts in recent years have brought bright prospects for China's educational advance. Statistics from 25 provinces, municipalities and autonomous regions show that more than 600 Chinese counties, 27 percent of the country's total, have in the main achieved universal primary school education, and large numbers of communes and brigades in other counties, have achieved this goal on their own. The blind development of general high schools has been stopped. Students in vocational schools in 1981 accounted for 23.8 percent of total senior secondary school enrolment. In 1979, it was 10 percent.

Full-time college enrolment more than doubled between 1976-1981, increasing from 565,000 to 1,280,000. Some

43,000 post-graduates were enrolled since that system was revived in 1978, 1.7 times the 1949-1966 total. Some 12,000 students were sent abroad for advanced study in recent years, and 4,000 foreign students were accepted by Chinese institutions. China today has nearly 10 million school teachers.

Apart from state universities, many factories, democratic parties and mass organizations are opening schools on their own.

四、练 习

一、替换练习：

1. 中国教育部长要求采取积极 | 措施 / 办法 | ，把人力资源转化 | 为 / 成 | 人才资源。

2. | 轻视 / 忽视 | 教育和科学的落后思想应该逐步得到 | 克服 / 解决 | 。

3. | 目前 / 当前 | 中国的教育事业在许多方面已经不能适应形势发展的 | 需要 / 要求 | 。

4．重大改革一定要经过 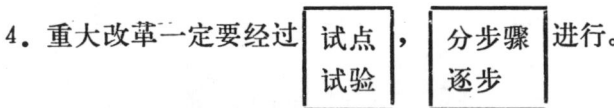 进行。

5．教育改革必须从 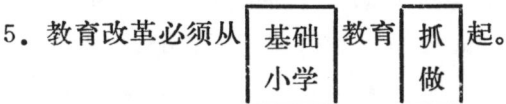 起。

6．现在， 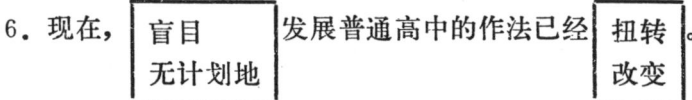 。

二、指出哪种解释符合句中划线部分词语的意思：
1．"教育是国家富强的基本条件之一"，这必须成为<u>人所共知</u>的常识。
　　（1）人们共同的知识
　　（2）大家都知道
　　（3）知道人和地点
2．重大改革一定要经过<u>试点</u>，分步骤进行。
　　（1）试验的地点
　　（2）试验的时间
　　（3）在一定的地方试验
3．高等教育的<u>学制要实行多层次</u>，办学形式要多样化。
　　（1）学校里有许多不同的年级
　　（2）学校里有不同的课程和学习年限
　　（3）学校有高低不同的领导机关
4．从1976年到1981年，全日制普通高等学校在校学生人数<u>翻了一番</u>。
　　（1）越来越多

(2) 增加一倍
(3) 转了一圈

三、解释下列各句中带"点"的词语：
1. 我们要采取积极措施把人力资源转化为丰富的人才资源。
2. 教育是国家富强的基本条件之一。
3. 要进一步发展电视、广播、函授教育，为提高干部、职工、教师和农民的文化科学水平服务。
4. 据不完全统计，现在已有600多个县基本普及了小学教育，约占全国总数的27%。
5. 最近五年来共招收研究生43,000多人，相当于1949年到1966年总数的170%。
6. 中国现在有近1,000万人的教师队伍。

四、熟悉下列词组：

1.
教育	事业
	体制
	制度
	结构
	改革

2.
采取	积极	措施
	有力	
	多种	

3.
基本	条件
	原则
	方针

4.
落后	思想
进步	
先进	
保守	
腐朽	

5.
小学	生
中学	
大学	
研究	
进修	
留学	

6.
基础	教育
中等	
高等	
业余	
职业	
成人	

五、阅　读

中国教育部长强调农村教育

新华社北京10月13日电　教育部长何东昌今天在接见亚太地区扫盲、成人教育实地考察讨论会代表时说，为了更好地发展中国的经济，首先是发展农业，要努力提高人口受教育的密度。

他解释说，十二大提出了二〇〇〇年实现工农业生产总产值翻两番的目标，并提出首先要发展农业、能源交通和教育科学。发展农业，只靠艰苦的体力劳动是不够的，还必须不断提高农民的文化水平，大力采用科学技术。自从实行生产责任制以后，农村已经出现了万元户，目前农民对科学技术的要求迫切了。

他强调指出，成人教育中很重要的一环是提高干部、首先是农村干部的文化水平。因为文化水平高的人更容易重视教育。但目前，教育的发展落后于经济发展。要开创教育事业的新局面，发动全社会重视教育，在基本学制的基础上，对农村要有较大的灵活性。高等教育要多层次多样化。今年有七万八千电大毕业生，还要采取措施增加。

他说，中国准备在一九九〇年普及小学教育。为此，要有步骤地发展学前教育。有条件的地方，包括富裕农村，要普及初级中学教育。

亚太地区扫盲、成人教育实地考察讨论会是十月四日在广东佛山开幕的。随后代表分两组去山东和河南考察，并于今天回到北京，进行总结讨论。

(1982 年)

生　词

1. 扫盲		sǎománg	eliminate illiteracy
2. 实地	(名)	shídì	on the spot
3. 考察	(动)	kǎochá	inspect; observe and study
4. 密度	(名)	mìdì	density
5. 解释	(动)	jiěshì	explain
6. 能源	(名)	néngyuán	the sources of energy
7. 局面	(名)	júmiàn	aspect; situation
8. 灵活性	(名)	línghuóxìng	flexibility; adaptability; mobility

专　名

1. 亚太地区	Yà-Tài Dìqū	the area of Asia and the Pacific

2. 佛山　　　　Fóshān　　　　地名

问　题

1. 中国教育部长接见了什么人，谈了什么问题？
2. 到2000年，中国提出了什么奋斗目标？
3. 教育部长为什么强调农村教育？
4. 他为什么说，首先要提高农村干部的文化水平？
5. 中国计划怎样改变教育落后于经济发展的现象？
6. 中国准备在什么时侯普及小学教育？

第 八 课

一、范 句

1. 计划 生育 工作 必须 为 国民 经济
   Jìhuà shēngyù gōngzuò bìxū wèi guómín jīngjì
   发展 服务。
   fāzhǎn fúwù
   The family planning work must serve the development of national economy.

2. 中国 政府 提倡 一 对 夫妇 只 生育
   Zhōngguó zhèngfǔ tíchàng yī duì fūfù zhǐ shēngyù
   一 个 孩子。
   yī gè háizi
   The Chinese Government advocates one child for one couple.

3. 他 肯定了 今年 计划 生育 工作 的
   Tā kěndìngle jīnnián jìhuà shēngyù gōngzuò de
   成绩。
   chéngjì
   He affirmed the achievements of the birth control work made in this year.

4. 今年 上半年 一胎率 比 去年 同期 略
   Jīnnián shàngbànnián yītāilǜ bǐ qùnián tóngqī lüè

有 提高。
yǒu tígāo

The one-child rate was slightly higher than the same period last year.

5. 宣传 部门 和 群众 团体 要 协助
Xuānchuán bùmén hé qúnzhòng tuántǐ yào xiézhù
计划 生育 委员会 做好 这 项 工作。
jìhuà shēngyù wěiyuánhuì zuòhǎo zhè xiàng gōngzuò

Propaganda departments and mass organizations should cooperate with the Family Planning Commision to do this work.

6. 在 今后 几 年 内 应 在 群众 中
Zài jīnhòu jǐ nián nei yīng zài qúnzhòng zhōng
普及 人口 理论 基本 知识。
pǔjí rénkǒu lǐlùn jīběn zhīshi

In the future years, the people should be better informed on basic knowledge of population theory.

7. 目前, 重男 轻女 的 封建 思想
Mùqián zhòng nán qīng nǚ de fēngjiàn sīxiǎng
仍然 存在。
réngrán cúnzài

At present, the feudal idea of regarding men as superior to women still exists.

8. 他 还 强调 要 加强 计划 生育 的
Tā hái qiángdiào yào jiāqiáng jìhuà shēngyù de
科研 工作。
kēyán gōngzuò

He also put stress on strenghtening of scientific research work on the family planning.

9. 每 个 人 都 应当 认识 到 计划 生育
   Měi gè rén dōu yīngdāng rènshi dào jìhuà shēngyù
   的 重 要 性。
   de zhòngyàoxìng

   Everyone should understand the importance of family planning.

10. 中 国 三十 岁 以下 的 人口 占 总
    Zhōngguó sānshí suì yǐxià de rénkǒu zhàn zǒng
    人口 的 百分 之 六十五。
    rénkǒu de bǎifēn zhī liùshíwǔ

    In China, 65 percent of the total population are under 30 years old.

11. 在 未来 的 十 多 年 中, 中国 人口
    Zài wèilái de shí duō nián zhong Zhōngguó rénkǒu
    的 增长 将 是 一 个 突出 的 问题。
    de zēngzhǎng jiāng shì yī gè tūchū de wèntí

    In the future 10 years or more, the population increase in China will be a predominant problem.

12. 到 本 世纪 末, 中 国 要 把 人口
    Dào běn shìjì mò Zhōngguó yào bǎ rénkǒu
    控制 在 十二 亿 内。
    kòngzhì zài shíèr yì nèi

    By the end of this century, China will control its population within 12 hundred million.

13. 他 对 实现 这 个 奋斗 目标 很 有
    Tā duì shíxiàn zhè gè fèndòu mùbiāo hěn yǒu
    信 心。
    xìnxīn

He was confident of fulfilling the struggling goal.

二、课 文

钱信忠再次强调计划生育

新华社北京8月10日电 国家计划生育委员会主任钱信忠今天说，计划生育工作必须为国民经济的发展服务，必须坚决地、严格地控制人口增长，提倡一对夫妇只生育一个孩子。

他肯定了今年上半年计划生育工作的成绩。他说，一胎率比去年同期略有提高，并且指出这是在去年新婚人数比前年大量增加的情况下取得的。

他要求宣传、新闻、文化、艺术、教育、卫生等各部门和妇联、工会、共青团等群众团体共同协助计划生育委员会做好这项工作。在今后几年内逐步做到在群众中普及避孕、节育知识，普及生理卫生常识，普及优生优育知识和人口理论基本知识。他批评说，目前重男轻女的封建思想仍然存在。

他还强调要加强计划生育的科研工作，搞好避孕药具的生产供应工作。避孕药具要简便、有效并保证供应。

他说，我国人口众多，30岁以下的人占总人口的65%，这预示着在未来十多年中，人口的增长将是一个很突出的问题。这就必须使人民认识到计划生育的必要性。

他最后很有信心地说，有政府和广大群众的共同努力，到二〇〇〇年把中国人口控制在十二亿内的奋斗目标完全可能实现。

(1982年)

三、生　词

1. 计划生育　　　　　jìhuà shēngyù　family planning
2. 控制　　　（动）　kòngzhì　　　　control
3. 提倡　　　（动）　tíchàng　　　　advocate; encourage
4. 一胎率　　（名）　yītāilǜ　　　　one-child rate (the rate of first-borns in the total births)
5. 新闻　　　（名）　xīnwén　　　　news
6. 妇联　　　（名）　fùlián　　　　the Women's Federation
7. 工会　　　（名）　gōnghuì　　　labour union
8. 共青团　　（名）　gòngqīngtuán　the Communist Youth League
9. 避孕　　　　　　　bìyùn　　　　contraception
10. 节育　　　　　　　jiéyù　　　　birth control
11. 普及　　　（动）　pǔjí　　　　popularize
12. 生理　　　（名）　shēnglǐ　　　physiology
13. 优生　　　（动）　yōushēng　　healther births
14. 封建思想　　　　　fēngjiàn sīxiǎng　feudal idea

15. 供应	（动）gōngyìng	supply
16. 简便	（形）jiǎnbiàn	simple and convenient
17. 突出	（形、动）tūchū	predominant; outstanding
18. 亿	（数）yì	a hundred million
19. 目标	（名）mùbiāo	objective; target; aim

专　名

1. 钱信忠　Qián Xìnzhōng　人名
2. 国家计划生育委员会　Guójiā Jìhuà Shēngyù Wěiyuánhuì
   the State Family Planning Commission

Translation

Qian Xinzhong Stress Family Planning

　　Beijing, August 10 (Xinhua) —Qian Xinzhong, Minister in Charge of the State Family Planning Commission, said here today that family planning work must serve the development of national economy, population must be controlled resolutely and rigidly and one-child family must be advocated.

　　He affirmed the achievements of the birth control work made in the first half of this year. He said that the first born rate was slightly higher than the same period last year.

He pointed out that this achievement was specially significant when taking into account of the fact that newly married couples in 1981 were more than that of 1980.

He called on the mass media, news, culture, art, education and health departments, trade unions as well as popular organizations of Women's Federation and Youth League to cooperate with the Family Planning Commission to do this work. In the future years, the people should be better informed on knowledge of contraception, physiology and hyginee, healthier births, child care and education, as well as basic knowledge of population theory. He criticized the present feudal idea preferring baby boys to girls still existed.

He also put stress on strenghtening of scientific research work on the family planning and also on the production and supply of contraceptives. There should be ample, effective and convenient contraceptives for the people.

Qian said that of China's very large population, 65 percent are under 30 years old, it means that population increase is a predominant problem in the future 10 years or more. So it is imperative that the people should understand the importance of family planning.

In his conclusion, he expressed confidence in fulfilling the struggling goal of controlling China's population within 12 hundred million by the year of 2000 through the combined efforts of the government and the masses.

四、练　习

一、替换练习：

1. 中国政府提倡 | 一对夫妇只生一个孩子 |。
　　　　　　　　| 计划生育 |
　　　　　　　　| 青年男女晚婚、晚育 |

2. 我国人口出生率比去年同期略有 | 提高 |。
　　　　　　　　　　　　　　　　| 增长 |
　　　　　　　　　　　　　　　　| 减少 |
　　　　　　　　　　　　　　　　| 下降 |

3. 在今后几年中，应在群众中普及 | 避孕、节育 | 知识。
　　　　　　　　　　　　　　　　| 生理卫生 |
　　　　　　　　　　　　　　　　| 人口理论 |

4. 目前，| 重男轻女的封建思想 | 仍然存在。
　　　　| 少数干部的特权思想 |
　　　　| 极左路线的错误影响 |

5. 每个人都应当认识到 | 计划生育 | 的重要性。
　　　　　　　　　　　| 发展教育事业 |
　　　　　　　　　　　| 建设精神文明 |

6. 他对 | 实现这个奋斗目标 | 很有信心。
　　　　 提前完成这个计划
　　　　 彻底解决这个问题

二、选词填空：

　　　　普及　　实现　　协助　　提倡
　　　　增长　　供应　　存在　　预示

1. 中国必须坚决地、严格地控制人口的_____。
2. 中国政府_____一对夫妇只生育一个孩子。
3. 宣传、教育、卫生等部门要_____计划生育委员会做好计划生育工作。
4. 为了搞好计划生育工作，必须在群众中_____避孕、节育、优生、优育的知识。
5. 避孕药具要简便、有效，并保证_____。
6. 中国人口众多，30岁以下的人占65%，这_____着在未来十年中人口的增长将是一个很突出的问题。
7. 目前，中国社会上重男轻女的现象仍然_____。
8. 我们一定努力_____这个奋斗目标，即到2000年把中国人口控制在12亿以内。

三、指出哪种解释符合句中划线部分词语的意思：

1. 中国政府<u>提倡</u>一对夫妇只生育一个孩子。
　　（1）一对夫妇只能生一个孩子
　　（2）一对夫妇最好只生一个孩子
　　（3）一对夫妇可以只生一个孩子
2. 今年一胎率比去年同期<u>略有提高</u>。
　　（1）有一点提高

(2) 有较大的提高
  (3) 大概有一些提高
3. 国家计划生育委员会主任指出，目前 重男轻女 的封建思想仍然存在。
  (1) 男的比女的重要
  (2) 男的重，女的轻
  (3) 重视男的，轻视女的
4. 我国人口众多，三十岁以下的人又占人口总数的65%，这预示着在未来的十多年中，人口增长将是一个 很突出 的问题。
  (1) 突破出来
  (2) 突然表现出来
  (3) 明显表现出来

四、熟悉下列词组：

1.
控制	人口（增长）
	局势
	军队
	宣传机器

2.
宣传	部门
文艺	
教育	
卫生	
商业	
政府	

3.
避孕节育	知识
生理卫生	
优生优育	
人口理论	
自然科学	
社会科学	

4.
加强	科研工作
	宣传工作
	思想教育
	党的领导
	团结合作

5.	保证	供应
		需要
		实现目标
		完成任务

6.	很有	信心
	满怀	
	充满	

五、阅 读

中国人口自然增长率下降

新华社北京10月27日电 一九八一年中国大陆二十九个省、市、自治区自然增加的人口为一千四百三十九万九千六百〇一人，自然增长率为千分之十四点五五。这是国家统计局今天在《关于一九八二年人口普查主要数字的公报》中公布的数字。这同一九六四年人口普查公布的千分之二十七点八的自然增长率相比，有明显的降低。人口自然增长率下降的根本原因是执行计划生育政策的结果。

胡耀邦总书记在刚结束的中共十二大报告中指出："实行计划生育，是我国的一项基本国策。"他提出："到本世纪末，必须力争把我国人口控制在十二亿以内。"这意味着在今后十八年内平均每年净增人口数必须控制在一千一百万以内。公报提供的人口普查统计数字表明，一九八一年中国大陆人口出生率为千分之二十点九一，而一九六四年为千分之三十九点三。

现在，全国已有一千六百多万对夫妇领取了独生子女证，有一亿多对育龄夫妇自觉地实行了避孕节育。中共中央和国务院今年三月发出的《关于进一步做好计划生育工作的指示》中，要求国家干部和职工、城镇居民除特殊情况外，一对夫妇只生一个孩子。在农村普遍提倡一对夫妇只生一个孩子。不论那种情况都不能生三胎。

一九八〇年统计，全国二十九个省、市、自治区中有十八个省市人口自然增长率下降到千分之十以下。与此同时，人口死亡率也在下降。公报公布的一九八一年中国大陆人口死亡率为千分之六点三六，而一九六四年为千分之十一点五。除生活条件改善的原因外，医疗卫生条件的改善是人口死亡率下降的重要原因。据卫生部在全国若干地区调查，一九八一年中国人口平均寿命为六十九岁，而在解放前只有三十五岁左右。

(1982年)

生 词

1. 自然增长率　zìrán zēngzhǎnglǜ　natural growth rate
2. 统计局　（名）tǒngjìjú　statistical bureau
3. 人口普查　　rénkǒu pǔchá　census
4. 世纪　（名）shìjì　century
5. 意味(着)　（动）yìwèi(zhe)　mean; imply; signify
6. 出生率　（名）chūshēnglǜ　birthrate

7.	独生子女		dúshēng zǐnǚ	only child
8.	育龄	（名）	yùlíng	child-bearing age
9.	死亡率	（名）	sǐwánglù	mortality rate
10.	因素	（名）	yīnsù	factor; element
11.	若干	（数）	ruògān	a certain of number or amount
12.	寿命	（名）	shòumìng	life; life-span

问 题

1. 1981年，中国人口自然增长率是多少？比从前上升了还是下降了？
2. 中国实行计划生育，控制人口增长的奋斗目标是什么？
3. 计划生育工作对育龄夫妇的具体要求是什么？
4. 许多夫妇领取了独生子女证，这是什么意思？
5. 当前，中国人口的出生率是多少？死亡率是多少？
6. 中国人口死亡率下降的主要原因是什么？
7. 中国人口平均寿命情况解放前后有什么变化？

第 九 课

一、范 句

1. 今年 上半年， 共 安置了 二百 四十 万 人 就业。
   Jīnnián shàngbànnián gòng ānzhìle èrbǎi sìshí wàn rén jiùyè.

   Two million and four hundred thousand people in China were assigned jobs in the first half of this year.

2. 在 城 镇 集体 所有制 企业 就业 的 人数 达 二千 五百 八十 八 万 人。
   Zài chéngzhèn jítǐ suǒyǒuzhì qǐyè jiùyè de rénshù dá èrqiān wǔbǎi bāshí bā wàn rén.

   The total number of workers in urban collective enterprises comes to 25.88 million.

3. 今年 上半年 还 安排了 一百 一十 万 人 从事 临时性 工作。
   Jīnnián shàngbànnián hái ānpáile yībǎi yīshí wàn rén cóngshì línshíxìng gōngzuò.

   In addition, 1.1 million people were assigned temporary jobs in the first half of this year.

4. 国家 鼓励 发展 集体 和 个体 经济，
   Guójiā gǔlì fāzhǎn jítǐ hé gètǐ jīngjì,

扩大 就业 门路。
kuòdà jiùyè ménlù.

The state encourages increased job opportunities by collective enterprises and self-employed businesses.

5. 为了 广开 就业 门路， 许多 地方 越来越
Wèile guǎngkāi jiùyè ménlù xǔduō dìfāng yuèláiyuè
注意 发展 集体 所有制 企业 和 个体
zhùyì fāzhǎn jítǐ shuǒyǒuzhì qǐyè hé gètǐ
企业。
qǐyè

Many places are paying more attention to establishing collective and individual businesses in order to open more channels for employment.

6. 许多 地方 建立了 劳动 服务 公司， 组织
Xǔduō dìfān jiànlìle láodòng fúwù gōngsī zǔzhī
待业 青年 进行 生产。
dàiyè qīngnián jìnxíng shēngchǎn

Many places set up labour service companies to organize job-waiting young people to start their own businesses.

7. 劳动 服务 公司 还 对 青年 进行
Láodòng fúwù gōngsī hái duì qīngnián jìnxíng
就业 训练。
jiùyè xùnliàn

The labor service companies also arrange technical training classes to prepare the young people for future work.

8. 据 劳动 人事部 统计， 目前 全 国
Jù láodòng rénshìbù tǒngjì mùqián quán guó

已 有 七千 六百 八十 六 个 劳动 服务
yǐ yǒu qīqiān liùbǎi bāshí liù gè láodòng fúwù
公司。
gōngsī

According to the Ministry of Labor and Personnel, there are 7,686 labor service companies in the whole country.

9. 它们 中 大 多数 是 由 企业、事业
Tāmen zhong dà duōshù shì yǒu qǐyè shìyè
单位 兴办 的。
dānwèi xīngbàn de

Most of them are run by enterprises and institutions.

10. 商业、 饮食、 服务 行业 发展 非常
Shāngyè yǐnshí fúwù hángyè fāzhǎn fēicháng
迅速。
xùnsù

The commercial, catering and service trades devoloped rapidly.

11. 劳动 人事部 号召 全面 贯彻 党
Láodòng rénshìbù hàozhào quánmiàn guànchè dǎng
和 国家 关于 就业 问题 的 决议。
hé guójiā guānyú jiùyè wèntí de juéyì

The Ministry of Labor and Personnel called on people to fully implement the Party and government decision on employment.

12. 集体 所有制 企业 使 许多 待业 青年
Jítǐ suǒyǒuzhì qǐyè shǐ xǔduō dàiyè qīngnián
得到了 就业 机会。
dédàole jiùyè jīhuì

The collective enterprises provide job opportunities for many job-waiting young people.

二、课　文

一九八二年上半年安置二百四十万人就业

新华社北京9月30日电 据劳动人事部新近提供的材料，今年上半年，二十八个省、市、自治区城镇共安置了二百四十万人就业。其中，全民所有制单位安排了二十万人，在集体所有制单位就业的有一百万人，从事个体经营的十万人。这样，在城镇集体所有制企业就业的人数达二千五百八十八万人，占全国就业总人数的百分之二十三点六。今年上半年还安排了一百一十万人从事临时性工作。

一九八一年十月十七日中共中央和国务院通过了一项决议，鼓励发展集体和个体经济，扩大就业门路。现在，企业正在进行结构调整。为了广开就业门路，许多地方越来越注意发展集体所有制企业和个体企业。

许多地方建立了劳动服务公司，组织待业青年进行生产，或负责安排青年在国营企业中临时就业。劳动服务公司还对青年进行就业训练。

据劳动人事部统计，目前全国已有七千六百八十六个劳动服务公司，它们中大多数是由企业、事业单位兴办的。由劳动服务公司安排就业训练的人数已达三百二十一万人。商业、饮食、服务行业的迅速发展，也使许多劳动力得到了就业机会。

劳动人事部号召继续全面贯彻党和国家关于就业问题的决议，努力打开发展集体所有制企业和个体经济就业的新局面。

(1982 年)

三、生　词

1.	安置	（动）	ānzhì	arrange for
2.	就业		jiùyè	employment
3.	自治区	（名）	zìzhìqū	autonomous region
4.	城镇	（名）	chéngzhèn	city and town
5.	全民所有制		quánmín suǒyǒuzhì	ownership by the whole people
6.	集体	（名）	jítǐ	collective
7.	个体	（名）	gètǐ	individual
8.	经营	（动）	jīngyíng	run; engage in
9.	临时性	（形）	línshíxìng	temporary
10.	决议	（名）	juéyì	dicision; resolution
11.	鼓励	（动）	gǔlì	encourage
12.	门路	（名）	ménlù	way
13.	企业	（名）	qǐyè	enterprise
14.	公司	（名）	gōngsī	company
15.	组织	（动）	zǔzhī	organize

16.	待业	dàiyè	job-waiting
17.	负责	(动) fùzé	be responsible for; be in charge of
18.	国营	guóyíng	state-owned
19.	训练	(动) xùnliàn	train
20.	统计	(动) tǒngjì	statistics
21.	事业单位	shìyè dānwèi	institution
22.	行业	(名) hángyè	trade
23.	号召	(动) hàozhào	call; appeal
24.	贯彻	(动) guànchè	implement

Translation

2.4 Million People in China Get Jobs

Beijing, September 30 (Xinhua) —Two million and four hundred thousand people in cities and towns in China got jobs in the first half of this year, according to statistics for 28 provinces, municipalities and autonomous regions provided by the Ministry of Labor and Personnel. While only 200,000 people of the newly employed were assigned jobs in state owned enterprises, one million were employed in collective enterprises and 100,000 were registered asself-employed. This brings the total number of workers in urban collective enterprises up to 25.88 million, accounting for 23.6 percent of the country's total employment. In addition 1.1 million got temporary jobs.

The state encourages increased job opportunities by collective enterprises and self-employed businesses, according to an October 17, 1981 decision issued by the Party Central committee and the State Council. While restructuring industrial enterprises, many places are paying more attention to establishing collective and individual businessess in order to open more channels for employment.

Many places set up labor service companies to orgaize job-waiting young people to start their own businesses or find temporary work in state-owned enterprises. The labor service companies also arrange technical training classes to prepare them for future work.

According to the Ministry of Labor and Personnel, there are 7,686 labor service companies in the whole country, most run by enterprises and institutions. The number of young people in training comes to 3.21 million. New progress was also made in the commercial, catering and service trades, and they also provided job opportunities.

The Ministry called on people to fully and continously implement the Party and government decision on employment and make energetic efforts to open up a new prospect of increase employment in collective and individual businesses.

四、练　习

一、替换练习：

1. 今年上半年，全国城镇共 | 安置 / 安排 | 了240万人 | 就业 / 参加工作 | 。

2. 半年里，又有 | 10万人 / 110万人 | 从事 | 个体经营 / 临时性工作 | 。

3. 中共中央和国务院通过一项决议，鼓励发展 | 集体 / 个体 | 经济， | 扩大 / 广开 | 就业门路。

4. 劳动服务公司对待业青年进行 | 就业训练 / 技术培训 | 。

5. 许多劳动服务公司是由 | 企业 / 事业 | 单位 | 兴办 / 举办 | 的。

6. | 商业
     饮食业
     服务行业 | 的发展，使许多城镇 | 劳动力
     待业青年
     待业人员 | 得到了就

业的机会。

二、把下列词语分别填入各句：

　　　　鼓励　　从事　　安置　　通过
　　　　兴办　　负责　　号召　　贯彻

1. 1982年上半年，二十八个省、市、自治区城镇共_____了240万人就业，其中有10万人_____个体经营。
2. 1981年10月党中央和国务院_____了一项关于就业问题的决议。
3. 劳动人事部门_____继续全面深入地_____这项决议，努力打开多种门路就业的新局面。
4. 现在中国采取多种措施_____发展商业、饮食业和服务行业。
5. 劳动服务公司除了对待业青年进行就业训练外，还_____安排他们在国营企业中从事临时性工作。
6. 许多劳动服务公司是由企业、事业单位_____的。

三、读出下列带有数字的句子：

1. 1982年上半年，全国城镇共安置2,400,000人就业。其中全民所有制安排了200,000人，在集体所有制就业的有1,000,000人，从事个体经营的有100,000人，从事临时性工作的有1,100,000人。
2. 目前，在城镇集体所有制工作的人数达到25,880,000人，占全国就业总人数的23.6%。

3. 现在全国已有7686个劳动服务公司,参加过就业训练的已达3,210,000人。
4. 据统计,1982年中国全国人口有1,031,882,511人,其中包括台湾省18,270,749人,港澳地区5,378,627人。

四、熟悉下列词组：

1. 安置　就业
　　　　工作
　　　　待业青年
　　　　劳动力

2. 就　业
　　从
　　待
　　失

3. 从事　集体经济
　　　　个体经营
　　　　临时性工作
　　　　教育事业
　　　　革命活动

4. 集体　所有制
　　　　经济
　　　　经营
　　　　活动

5. 全民　所有制
　　集体
　　个体

6. 据…　统计
　　　　计算
　　　　报道
　　　　消息

7. 贯彻　决议
　　　　方针
　　　　政策
　　　　会议精神

五、阅　读

受人们欢迎的劳动服务公司

新华社北京 10 月 22 日电　到一九八一年底，全国各地劳动服务公司已安置和培训了三百二十一万待业人员，深受广大群众和社会的欢迎。

据国家劳动总局统计，在这些人员中，中学毕业生占百分之九十五。他们有的已在劳动服务公司举办的企业事业单位就业，有的参加了劳动服务公司组织的临时工队伍，有的正在就业训练班学习。

目前，中国共有七千六百八十六所劳动服务公司，分布在二十八个省、市、自治区。其中三分之一是县以上的劳动服务部门办的，三分之二是企业事业单位办的。

各地的劳动服务公司根据本地区的条件和社会的需要，组织各种形式的专业服务队，从事修理、饮食服务、房屋维修、搬运、城市绿化、幼儿托育等工作，或者成立加工厂或车间，拾遗补缺、修旧利废。

随着我国电子工业的发展，许多家庭购买了电视机和其他家用电器，但维修服务供不应求。各地劳动服务公司根据这一情况，增设了电视机和家用电器维修门市部，并培训了一批修理人员。

劳动服务公司还在居民点开设理发店、缝纫店和代销店，为居民提供方便。这些集体经济单位是按照自愿

3. 现在全国已有7686个劳动服务公司，参加过就业训练的已达3,210,000人。
4. 据统计，1982年中国全国人口有1,031,882,511人，其中包括台湾省18,270,749人，港澳地区5,378,627人。

四、熟悉下列词组：

1. 安置 ｜ 就业
       工作
       待业青年
       劳动力

2. 就 ｜ 业
   从
   待
   失

3. 从事 ｜ 集体经济
       个体经营
       临时性工作
       教育事业
       革命活动

4. 集体 ｜ 所有制
       经济
       经营
       活动

5. 全民 ｜ 所有制
   集体
   个体

6. 据… ｜ 统计
       计算
       报道
       消息

7. 贯彻 ｜ 决议
       方针
       政策
       会议精神

五、阅 读

受人们欢迎的劳动服务公司

新华社北京10月22日电 到一九八一年底，全国各地劳动服务公司已安置和培训了三百二十一万待业人员，深受广大群众和社会的欢迎。

据国家劳动总局统计，在这些人员中，中学毕业生占百分之九十五。他们有的已在劳动服务公司举办的企业事业单位就业，有的参加了劳动服务公司组织的临时工队伍，有的正在就业训练班学习。

目前，中国共有七千六百八十六所劳动服务公司，分布在二十八个省、市、自治区。其中三分之一是县以上的劳动服务部门办的，三分之二是企业事业单位办的。

各地的劳动服务公司根据本地区的条件和社会的需要，组织各种形式的专业服务队，从事修理、饮食服务、房屋维修、搬运、城市绿化、幼儿托育等工作，或者成立加工厂或车间，拾遗补缺、修旧利废。

随着我国电子工业的发展，许多家庭购买了电视机和其他家用电器，但维修服务供不应求。各地劳动服务公司根据这一情况，增设了电视机和家用电器维修门市部，并培训了一批修理人员。

劳动服务公司还在居民点开设理发店、缝纫店和代销店，为居民提供方便。这些集体经济单位是按照自愿组合、自负盈亏、按劳分配、民主管理的原则办起来的。

　　劳动服务公司不仅把待业人员组织起来，按照社会需要，开辟新的生产服务门路，而且还举办了各种就业培训班，在过去的两年中，培训了五十多万人。

（1982 年）

生　词

1. 培训　　　　（动）péixùn　　　　train
2. 毕业生　　　（名）bìyèshēng　　graduate
3. 分布　　　　（动）fēnbù　　　　be distributed; be scattered
4. 县　　　　　（名）xiàn　　　　　county
5. 修理　　　　（动）xiūlǐ　　　　repair; mend
6. 维修　　　　（动）wéixiū　　　keep in (good) repair; maintain
7. 搬运　　　　（动）bānyùn　　　carry; transport
8. 绿化　　　　（名、动）lǜhuà　　afforest
9. 幼儿托育　　　　yòuér tuōyù　child-care
10. 加工　　　　（动）jiāgōng　　process
11. 拾遗补缺　　　shíyí-bǔquē　　make good omissions and deficiencies
12. 修旧利废　　　xiūjiù-lìfèi　　repair and utilize old or discarded things
13. 电子　　　　（名）diànzǐ　　　electron
14. 供不应求　　　gōng bù yìng qiú　supply falls short of demand; demand exceeds supply

15.	门市部	(名)	ménshìbù	retail department; sales department
16.	代销店	(名)	dàixiāodiàn	commission agent; shop commissioned to sell certain goods
17.	自负盈亏		zì fù yíng-kuī	(of an enterprise) assume sole resposibility for its profits or losses
18.	开辟	(动)	kāipì	open up; start

问 题

1. 劳动服务公司是作什么的？
2. 目前中国有多少劳动服务公司？经过它安置和培训的有多少人？
3. 劳动服务公司是由谁举办的？
4. 劳动服务公司从事的服务工作有哪些？
5. 公司为什么大力培训电器维修人员？
6. 什么是代销店？有什么作用？
7. 集体企业的经营管理原则是什么？
8. 劳动服务公司对解决就业问题有什么意义？

第 十 课

一、范 句

1. 西藏　出现了　三十　多　年　来　少　有　的　好　形势。
   Xīzàng chūxiànle sānshí duō nián lái shǎo yǒu de hǎo xíngshì

   An excellent situation rarely seen in the past 30 years or more has materialized in Tibet.

2. 这　个　成绩　的　取得　是　由于　贯彻了　中央　人民　政府　制定　的　对　西藏　的　新　政策。
   Zhè gè chéngjì de qǔdé shì yóuyú guànchèle zhōngyāng rénmín zhèngfǔ zhìdìng de duì Xīzàng de xīn zhèngcè

   The success was attributed to the implementation of the new policies for Tibet adopted by the central people's government.

3. 藏族　有　同　其他　民族　完全　平等　的　政治　地位。
   Zàngzú yǒu tóng qítā mínzú wánquán píngděng de zhèngzhì dìwèi

   The Tibetan nationality has equal political status with other nationalities.

4. 多数　地方　各　级　政府　领导　都　由
   Duōshù dìfāng gè jí zhèngfǔ lǐngdǎo dōu yóu
   藏族　干部　担任。
   Zàngzú gànbù dānrèn

   Most leaders of the local governments are Tibetan cadres.

5. 现在　的　干部　绝　大　多数　是　在
   Xiànzài de gànbù jué dà duōshù shì zài
   一九五九　年　民主　改革　以后　成长　起来
   yījiǔwǔjiǔ nián mínzhǔ gǎigé yǐhòu chéngzhǎng qǐlái
   的。
   de

   The overwhelming majority of the government officials today are new faces who have come to the fore since the 1959 democratic reform.

6. 这些　干部　了解　群众　的　愿望，　能
   Zhèxiē gànbù liǎojiě qúnzhòng de yuànwàng néng
   倾听　群众　的　呼声。
   qīngtīng qúnzhòng de hūshēng

   These cadres understand the aspirations of the people and can listen carefully to their demands.

7. 各　级　政府　领导人　都　是　通过　群众
   Gè jí zhèngfǔ lǐngdǎorén dōu shì tōngguò qúnzhòng
   选举　产生　的。
   xuǎnjǔ chǎnshēng de

   The government leaders at defferent levels are all elected by the masses.

8. 西藏 人民 从来 没有 象 今天 这样
   Xīzàng rénmín cónglái méiyǒu xiàng jīntiān zhèyàng
   充分 行使 当家 作主 的 权力。
   chōngfèn xíngshǐ dāngjiā zuòzhǔ de quánlì

   The Tibetans have never enjoyed such full rights as masters of their own region as today.

9. 自从 一九八〇 年 放宽 政策 以来，
   Zìcóng yījiǔbālíng nián fàngkuān zhèngcè yǐlái
   农 牧业 生产 获得 迅速 发展， 群众
   nóng-mùyè shēngchǎn huòdé xùnsù fāzhǎn qúnzòng
   的 生活 有 了 明显 改善。
   de shēnghuó yǒu le míngxiǎn gǎishàn

   Since the adoption of the flexible policies in 1980, Tibet has reported rapid growth in agriculture and stockbreeding, the people's living standards have improved markedly.

10. 随着 生产 的 发展， 农 牧民 的 收入
    Suízhe shēngchǎn de fāzhǎn nóng-mùmín de shōurù
    大幅度 增加。
    dàfúdù zēngjiā

    The income of both peaasnts and herdsmen has increased greatly with the development of production.

11. 西藏 群众 的 风俗 习惯 和 宗教
    Xīzàng qúnzhòng de fēngsú xíguàn hé zōngjiào
    信仰 都 得到 充分 尊重， 传统 的
    xìnyǎng dōu dédào chōngfèn zūnzhòng chuántǒng de
    文化 得到 恢复 和 发展。
    wénhuà dédào huīfù hé fāzhǎn

The Tibetans' customs, habits and religious beliefs have been fully respected, traditional culture has been restored and developed.

12. 中央 政府 和 各 兄弟 省 市 对 藏族
    Zhōngyāng zhèngfǔ hé gè xiōngdì shěng-shì duì Zàngzú
    人民 非常 关心， 并 给予 很 大 支持。
    rénmín fēicháng guānxīn bìng jǐyǔ hěn dà zhīchí

    The central government, brother provinces and municipalities have paid kind attention to Tibetans and given great support.

13. 西藏 农牧民 享受 免费 医疗、 免费
    Xīzàng nóng-mùmín xiǎngshòu miǎnfèi yīliáo miǎnfèi
    看 电影、 孩子 免费 上学 等 各 种
    kàn diànyǐng háizi miǎnfèi shàngxué děng gèzhǒng
    优待。
    yōudài

    Tibetan peasants and herdsmen enjoy many special treatment such as free medical treatment, free film shows and free schooling for children.

14. 西藏 的 命运 同 祖国 的 命运 紧紧
    Xīzàng de mìngyùn tóng zǔguó de mìngyùn jǐnjǐn
    联系 在 一起。
    liánxì zài yīqǐ

    The fate of Tibet is closely linked with that of the motherland;

15. 藏族 只有 在 祖国 的 大 家庭 中，
    Zàngzú zhǐyǒu zài zǔguó de dà jiātíng zhong

才 有 光 明 的 前途。
cái yǒu guāngmíng de qiántú

Only in the big family of the motherland can Tibetans have a bright future.

二、课　文

西藏领导干部赞扬党的民族政策

新华社拉萨 8 月 12 日电　全国人大常委会副委员长、西藏自治区人民政府主席阿沛·阿旺晋美最近对新华社记者说，"现在全区政治安定，群众安居乐业，出现了三十多年来少有的好形势。"

阿沛说，这个成绩的取得是由于贯彻了中央人民政府在 1980 年制定的对西藏的新政策。

他说，在祖国各民族大家庭中，我们藏族有同其他民族完全平等的政治地位。在全国人大常委会的 19 个副委员长中有两名藏族副委员长，在党和国家机关中也有一批藏族负责人。

他指出，最近几年，西藏的民族区域自治大大加强了。现在藏族和其他少数民族干部已占全区干部总数的百分之五十四以上，自治区各级人大常委会主任和各级政府的第一把手，已全由藏族和其他少数民族干部担任。现在的干部绝大部分是 1959 年民主改革后成长起来的，他们了解群众的愿望，能倾听群众的呼声。阿沛说："现在各级政府领导人都是通过群众选举产生的。我感到,西藏人民从来没有象今天这样充分行使当家作主的权力。"

阿沛谈到了两年来西藏经济的变化。他说:"自从1980年放宽经济政策以来,农牧业生产获得迅速发展,群众的生活有了明显改善。1981年全区农牧业总产值达到48,700万元,比1979年增长19.5%。粮食总产量达到483,500吨,比1979年增加60,500吨。随着生产的发展、农牧业税的免除和农畜产品收购价格的提高,农牧民的收入大幅度增加,全区农牧民人均收入由1979年的127元提高到200元。

阿沛列举了大量事实说明,中央和各兄弟省、市对藏族人民非常关心,对西藏给予很大的支持,以促进西藏经济文化的发展。1980年至1982年,中央政府给西藏的财政补助达16亿多元,占西藏财政支出的98%。西藏农牧民享受着免费医疗、免费看电影、孩子免费上学等各种优待。

他接着谈到,现在藏族群众的风俗习惯和宗教信仰都得到了充分尊重,传统的藏族文化得到了恢复和发展。不管走到哪里,都可以看到,藏族群众心情舒畅,喜气洋洋。

他说:"西藏的命运是同祖国的命运紧紧联系在一起的,藏族只有在祖国大家庭中才有光明的前途。"

(1982年)

三、生 词

1.	安居乐业		ān jū lè yè	live and work in peace and contentment
2.	第一把手		dìyībǎshǒur	number one man; first in **command**
3.	倾听	(动)	qīngtīng	listen attentively to
4.	呼声	(名)	hūshēng	cry; voice
5.	选举	(动)	xuǎnjǔ	elect
6.	行使	(动)	xíngshǐ	exercise; perform
7.	放宽	(动)	fàngkuān	relax restrictions
8.	总产值		zǒngchǎnzhí	total output value
9.	总产量		zǒngchǎnliàng	total output
10.	免除	(动)	miǎnchú	remit; excuse; relieve
11.	税	(名)	shuì	tax
12.	收购	(动)	shōugòu	purchase; buy
13.	大幅度		dàfúdù	a big margin; greatly
14.	人均收入		rénjūn shōurù	average per-capita income
15.	风俗	(名)	fēngsú	customs
16.	宗教	(名)	zōngjiào	religion
17.	信仰	(名、动)	xìnyǎng	belief; faith
18.	列举	(动)	lièjǔ	cite; list; enumerate
19.	事实	(名)	shìshí	fact
20.	给予	(动)	jǐyǔ	give; grant
21.	享受	(动)	xiǎngshòu	enjoy
22.	免费		miǎnfèi	free of charge
23.	医疗	(动)	yīliáo	medical treatment

24. 优待　　（动）yōudài　　give preferential treatment
25. 命运　　（名）mìngyùn　　fate

专　名

1. 西藏　　　　　Xīzàng　　　　Tibet
2. 阿沛·阿旺晋美　Āpèi·Āwàngjìnměi

人名

3. 藏族　　　　　Zàngzú　　　　Tibetan nationality

Translation

Tibetan Leader Praise Party's Nationalities Policy

Lhasa, August 12 (Xinhua) — "An excellent situation rarely seen in the past 30 years or more has materialized in Tibet. It is characterized by politaicl stability and a much better life of the people," said Ngapoi Ngawang Jigme, Vice-Chairman of the Standing Committee of the National People's Congress and Chairman of the Tibet Autonomous Regional People's Government, in an interview with Xinhua.

Ngapoi attributed the success to the implementation of the new policies for Tibet adopted by the central government in 1980.

He said in the big family of unitary multination motherland, the Tibetan nationality has equal political status with other nationalities. Among the 19 Vice-Chairmen of the N.P.C. Standing Committee, are two tibetans. A number of tibetans have taken up leading posts in the Party and state organs.

He said in recent years Tibet has gained greater regional autonomy. More than 54 percent of the government officials are drawn from among the region's Tibetan and other minority nationalities. All the leaders of the local governments and chairmen of the people's congress standing committees are Tibetans and other minority nationalities. The overwhelming majority of the government officials are new faces who have come to the fore since the 1959 democratic reform in Tibet. They understand the aspirations of the people and can listen carefully to their demands. He said "the government leaders at all levels are all elected by the masses. The Tibetans have never enjoyed such full rights as masters of their own region as today."

Ngapoi is gratified with the tremendous economic changes in the region in the past two years.

"Since the adoption of the flexible policies in 1980, Tibet has reported rapid growths in agriculture and stockbreeding. The people's living standards have improved markedly. In 1981, total output value of agriculture and stockbreeding was reached 487 million yuan, 19.5 percent more than 1979. Grain output was 483,500 tons, 60,500 tons more than 1979. The income of both peasants and herdsmen has increased greatly with the development of production, exemption of taxes and the rise in state purchase prices of farm produce.

The average per-capita income has risen from 127 yuan in 1979 to 200 yuan last year." he said.

He cited many facts to show the kind attention and support given by the central government, brother provinces and municipalities throughout the country to promote economic and cultural development in Tibet. Between 1980 and 1982 the region received 1.6 billion yuan in subsidies from the central government, accounting for 98 percent of the region's expenditure. Tibetan peasants and herdsmen enjoy free medical treatment, free film shows and free schooling for children.

Ngapoi said the Tibetans' customs, habits and religious beliefs have been fully respected. Traditional culture has been restored and developed. "Everywhere you go, you can see the masses have ease of mind and are elated with joy."

"The fate of Tibet is closely linked with that of the motherland. Only in the big family of the motherland can our region have a bright future," he said.

四、练 习

一、替换练习：

1. 西藏自治区出现了三十多年来少有的 | 好形势 | 。
   | 大好局面 |
   | 新气象 |

2. 地方各级政府的 {领导 / 负责人 / 第一把手} 都由藏族干部担任。

3. 随着 {生产的发展 / 农牧税的免除 / 农畜产品收购价格的提高}，农牧民的收入 {大幅度 / 大量 / 明显} 增加。

4. 藏族群众的 {风俗习惯 / 宗教信仰 / 传统文化} 得到了充分尊重。

5. 西藏农牧民享受着免费 {医疗 / 上学 / 看电影} 的优待。

6. {西藏 / 藏族人民} 的命运是同 {祖国 / 祖国各族人民} 的命运紧紧地联系在一起的。

二、填入适当的字组成动词，完成句子：

1. 中央人民政府在1980年____定了对西藏的新政策。

2. 在西藏地区，许多民族干部＿＿任了各级政府的领导工作。
3. 一个好干部必须了解群众的愿望，＿＿听群众的呼声。
4. 现在，各级政府的领导人都是通过群众＿＿举产生的。
5. 西藏人民从来没有象今天这样充分＿＿使当家作主的权力。
6. 随着生产的迅速发展，人民群众的生活有了明显改＿＿。
7. 绝大部分西藏的财政支出由中央政府补＿＿。
8. 为了说明这个问题，他＿＿举了大量事实。

三、指出哪种解释符合句中划线部分词语的意思：
1. 西藏全区政治安定，群众安居乐业，出现了<u>三十多年来少有的</u>好形势。
    (1) 三十多年来曾有过，但不多见
    (2) 三十多年来差不多没有过
    (3) 三十多年来虽然有过，但时间很短
2. 自治区各级政府的<u>第一把手</u>已全部由藏族或其他少数民族干部担任。
    (1) 最能干的人
    (2) 最老的领导人
    (3) 领导中第一位负责人
3. 全区农牧民<u>人均</u>收入由1979年的127元提高到200元。
    (1) 每人同样收入
    (2) 每人平均收入
    (3) 每人全部收入
4. 现在不管走到<u>哪里</u>，都可以看到群众喜气洋洋。
    (1) 指某一个地方
    (2) 指任何一个地方

(3) 指不清楚的地方

四、熟悉下列词组：

1. | 民族 | 政策 |
	（区域）自治
	大家庭
	平等
	团结
	解放运动

2. | 贯彻 | 政策 |
执行	
实行	
采取	
制定	
放宽	

3. | 大幅度 | 增加 |
	增长
	提高
	上升
	下降
	波动

4. | 列举 | 大量 | 事实 |
		事例
		数字
		材料
		证据

5. | 财政 | 支出 |
	收入
	补助
	赤字

6. | 尊重 | 风俗习惯 |
	宗教信仰
	民族自治权
	国家主权

五、阅　读

西藏妇女的作用

新华社拉萨9月7日电　目前，西藏自治区共有妇女干部八千多名，占全区干部总数的百分之三十点八五。

这是全国妇联副主席、西藏自治区妇联名誉主席阿沛·才旦卓嘎在最近召开的自治区第三次妇女代表大会上对记者宣布的。

她说，西藏的妇女已成为建设新西藏的一支重要力量。但是，在一九五九年西藏实行民主改革之前的封建农奴制统治下，广大的西藏妇女被视为"最卑贱的人"。她们没有任何人身自由。

她说，民主改革以后，为了培养妇女干部，每年都有大批妇女被送到各地开办的训练班、读书班学习文化和科学知识，有的还被送到内地的高等院校深造。现在，在自治区党委、人民政府、人大常委会以及各地、县领导机构中，均有女干部担任领导职务。他们当中不少人被选为中国共产党全国代表大会代表、全国人民代表大会代表和各种全国性重要会议的代表。

她说，西藏妇女不但在农业和畜牧业生产上发挥了重要作用，同时，随着工业的发展，西藏第一代妇女工人队伍已成长起来了。她们当中有优秀的女矿工、女技术员、女工程师、女司机等。目前，全区已涌现出"三八"红旗集体六十五个。

(1982年)

生　词

1. 名誉主席　　　　　míngyù zhǔxí　honourary president
2. 农奴制　　（名）nóngnúzhì　　system of serfdom
3. 统治　　　（动）tǒngzhì　　　rule; dominate
4. 卑贱　　　（形）bēijiàn　　　lowly
5. 训练班　　（名）xùnliànbān　 training course
6. 内地　　　（名）nèidì　　　　interior; inland
7. 深造　　　（动）shēnzào　　　take a more advanced course of study or training
8. 职务　　　（名）zhíwù　　　　post; duties; job
9. 矿工　　　（名）kuànggōng　　miner
10. 工程师　　（名）gōngchéngshī engineer
11. 司机　　　（名）sījī　　　　driver
12. 涌现　　　（动）yǒngxiàn　　 emerge in large numbers; spring up

问　题

1. 目前，西藏自治区有多少妇女干部？占干部总数的多少？
2. 1959年西藏民主改革前，西藏妇女的地位如何？现在有什么变化？
3. 民主改革后，怎样培养妇女干部？
4. 什么是"三八"红旗集体？
5. 为什么说西藏妇女已成为建设新西藏的一支重要力量？

第十一课

一、范句

1. 经过 三 年 多 的 调整, 中国 国民 经济 出现了 协调 发展 的 新 局面。
   Jīngguò sān nián duō de tiáozhěng, Zhōngguó guómín jīngjì chūxiànle xiétiáo fāzhǎn de xīn júmiàn.
   Following over three years of readjustment, China's national economy shows new situation of harmonious development.

2. 为了 加快 农业 和 轻工业 的 发展, 中央 采取了 一系列 措施 和 政策。
   Wèile jiākuài nóngyè hé qīnggōngyè de fāzhǎn, zhōngyāng cǎiqǔle yīxìliè cuòshī hé zhèngcè.
   In order to speed up the growth of agriculture and light industry, the central authorities adopted a series of measures and policies.

3. 自 一九七九 年 以来, 放慢了 一些 重工业 部门 的 发展 速度。
   Zì yījiǔqījiǔ nián yǐlái, fàngmànle yīxiē zhònggōngyè bùmén de fāzhǎn sùdù.
   Since 1979 the growing speed of some sectors of the heavy industry was restrained.

4. 在 过去 三 年 中， 农业 总产值 平均
   Zài guòqù sān nián zhōng nóngyè zǒngchǎnzhí píngjūn
   每年 递增 百分之 五点六。
   měinián dìzēng bǎifēn zhī wǔ diǎnr liù

   In the last three years, total agricultural output value showed an average annual growth rate of 5.6 percent.

5. 由于 片面 强调 重工业 优先 发展，
   Yóuyú piànmiàn qiángdiào zhònggōngyè yōuxiā fāzhǎn
   结果 造成 国民 经济 各 部门 失调。
   jiéguǒ zàochéng guómín jīngjì gè bùmén shītiáo

   The lopsided emphasis on heavy industry resulted in disproportionate development of the various sectors of the national economy

6. 在 工农业 总产值 中， 农业、轻工业
   Zài gōng-nóngyè zǒngchǎnzhí zhōng nóngyè qīnggōngyè
   所占的 比重 上升 到 百分之
   suǒ zhàn de bǐzhòng shàngshēng dào bǎifēnzhī
   六十三 点 五， 重工业 所 占 的
   liùshísān diǎnr wǔ zhònggōngyè suǒ zhàn de
   比重 下降 到 百分 之 三十六 点 五。
   bǐzhòng xiàjiàng dào bǎifēn zhī sānshíliù diǎnr wǔ

   Agriculture and light industry rose to account for 63.5 percent of the gross agricultural and industrial output value, the proportion taken by heavy industry dropped to 36.5 percent.

7. 轻工业 部门 生产 出了 更 多 的 人民
   Qīnggōngyè bùmén shēngchǎnchūle gèng duō de rénmín

生活 需要 的 产品。
shēnghuó xūyào de chǎnpǐn

The light industry turned out more products needed by the people's life.

8. 粮食 生产 稳步 增长, 棉花 和 家禽
Liángshi shēngchǎn wěnbù zēngzhǎng miánhuā hé jiāqín
的 增长 幅度 更 大 一些。
de zēngzhǎng fúdù gèng dà yīxiē

Grain production has been rising steadily, with still bigger increases in cotton and poultry.

9. 当前 市场 繁荣 是 三十 多 年
Dāngqián shìchǎng fánróng shì sānshí duō nián
来 所 少见 的。
lái suǒ shǎojiàn dè

At present the brickness of the market is rarely seen in the last 30 years.

10. 许多 食品 和 日用 工业品 已 敞开
Xǔduō shípǐn hé rìyòng gōngyèpǐn yǐ chǎngkāi
供应。
gōngyìng

Rationing has been lifted on many foodstuffs and manufactured goods for daily use.

11. 农业 生产 增长 为 轻工业 提供了
Nóngyè shēngchǎn zēngzhǎng wèi qīnggōngyè tígōngle
更 多 的 原料。
gèng duō de yuánliào

The growth of agriculture has provided more raw materials for light industry.

12. 农业、 轻工业 的 发展 为 重工业 发展
    Nóngyè qīnggōngyè de fāzhǎn wèi zhònggōngyè fāzhǎn
    打下 坚实 的 基础。
    dǎxià jiānshí de jīchǔ

The growth of agriculture and light industry has provided a more solid base for heavy industrial growth.

二、课 文

中国国民经济出现协调发展的局面

新华社北京 8 月 9 日电 中国国民经济经过三年多的调整，农业、轻工业和重工业等主要经济部门开始出现协调发展的局面。

自一九七九年国民经济开始调整以来，党中央和国务院采取了一系列措施和政策，加快农业和轻工业的发展，放慢了一些重工业部门的发展速度。

从一九七九年到一九八一年的三年中，中国农业总产值平均每年递增百分之五点六，轻工业递增百分之十四，是一九五二年以来增长速度最快的（一九五二年是一九四九年中国解放以来进行三年经济恢复时期的最后一年）。从一九七九年到一九八一年期间，重工业平均每年递增百分之一点四。

过去，由于片面强调重工业优先发展，结果造成国民经济各部门比例失调，使一些日用工业品和肉、蛋等

副食品供应不足。

去年，农业、轻工业在工农业总产值中所占的比重，已由一九七八年的百分之五十七点四上升到百分之六十三点五，而重工业所占的比重则相应地由百分之四十二点六下降到百分之三十六点五。

轻工业和重工业部门生产出更多人民生活和社会主义建设需要的适销对路的产品。粮食生产稳步增长，棉花、油料、糖料、家禽和猪牛羊肉的增长幅度更大一些。林、牧、副、渔在农业总产值中的比重，由一九七八年的百分之三十二点二，上升到一九八一年的百分之三十五点九。

当前市场繁荣是建国三十多年来所少见的。食品和日用工业品供应充足。许多原来凭票供应的商品，已变为敞开供应。

农业生产增长已为轻工业提供更多的原料，轻工业发展又为基本建设提供了更多的资金。农业、轻工业的发展为重工业发展打下坚实的基础。一九八一年重工业曾下降，今年一至七月份重工业总产值增长百分之九点七。

(1982年)

三、生　词

1. 国民经济　　　　　guómín jīngjì　national economy
2. 调整　　　（动）　tiáozhěng　　　readjust
3. 农业　　　（名）　nóngyè　　　　agriculture
4. 轻工业　　（名）　qīnggōngyè　　light industry

5.	重工业	(名)	zhònggōngyè	heavy industry
6.	协调	(形、动)	xiétiáo	coordinate
7.	一系列		yīxìliè	a series
8.	速度	(名)	sùdù	speed
9.	递增		dìzēng	increase by degrees; increase progressively
10.	片面	(形)	piànmiàn	lopsided; one-sided
11.	失调		shītiáo	dislocation
12.	副食品	(名)	fùshípǐn	non-staple food
13.	比重	(名)	bǐzhòng	proportion
14.	相应	(副)	xiāngyìng	corresponding; relevant
15.	适销对路		shìxiāo duìlù	meet the need of customer
16.	家禽	(名)	jiāqín	domestic fowl; poultry
17.	幅度	(名)	fúdù	range; scope; extent
18.	林(业)	(名)	lín(yè)	forestry
19.	牧(业)	(名)	mù(yè)	animal husbandry
20.	副(业)	(名)	fù(yè)	sideline
21.	渔(业)	(名)	yú(yè)	fishery
22.	市场	(名)	shìchǎng	market
23.	繁荣	(形)	fánróng	flourishing; prosperous
24.	凭票供应		píngpiào gōngyìng	supply by coupons
25.	敞开	(动)	chǎngkāi	open wide; unlimited
26.	基本建设		jīběn jiànshè	capital construction
27.	资金	(名)	zījīn	fund

Translation

China's National Economy Shows More Harmonious Development

Beijing, August 9 (Xinhua) — Following over three years of economic readjustment, the principal sectors of China's economy — agriculture, light industsy and heavy industry — come to show new situation of coordinated development.

Since the readjustment of national econumy started in 1979, the Central Committee of the Party and State Council adopted a series of measures and policies to speed up the growth of agriculture and light industry and restrain the pace of some sectors of the heavy industry.

In the three years from 1979-1981, total agricultural output value showed an average annual growth rate of 5.6 percent, light industry rose at an annual rate of 14 percent; Both showed the highest growth rate since 1952, at the end of the three-year rehabilitation of the national economy following China's liberation in 1949. Heavy industry increased at an average annual rate of 1.4 percent between 1979 and 1981.

Prior to this, the lopsided emphasis on heavy industry resulted in disproportionate development of the various sectors of the national economy and inadequate supply of some manufactured goods and meat, eggs and other non-staple food.

Agriculture and light industry last year rose to account for 63.5 percent of the gross agricultural and industrial output value as against 57.4 percent in 1978. The proportion taken up by heavy industry dropped from the 42.6 percent in 1978 to 36.5 percent.

The light and heavy industries turned out more products needed by the people's life and socialist construction. Grain production has been rising steadily, with still bigger increases in cotton, oil-bearing crops, sugarbeet and sugarcane, poultry, pork, beef and mutton. The percentage of forestry, animal husbandry, fishery and other sidelines in the gross agricultural output value rose to 35.9 percent in 1981 as compared with 32.2 percent in 1978.

The brickness of the home market is about the best in the last 30 years. Supply of foodstuffs and manufactured goods for daily use is ample. Rationing has been lifted on many goods that used to be available in limited quantities.

The growth of agriculture has provided more raw materials for light industry, which in turn, has turned out more profit for undertaking capital construction. The growth of these two sectors of the national economy has provided a more solid base for heavy industrial growth. China's heavy industry, which dropped in 1981, rose by 9.7 percent in the first seven months of this year.

四、练　习

一、替换练习：

1. 经过三年多的调整，中国的 { 主要经济部门 / 农业与工业 / 轻工业与重工业 } 开始出现了协调发展的新局面。

2. 中国采取了一系列 { 措施 / 政策 / 办法 }，加快农业和轻工业的发展。

3. 最近三年来，中国轻工业的总产值平均每年 { 递增 / 增加 / 增长 / 上升 } 14%。

4. { 农业、轻工业 / 林、牧、副、渔业 / 轻工业 } 在 { 工农 / 农业 / 工业 } 总产值中所占的比重已经明显上升。

5. | 农业生产的增长　|　为　| 轻工业　| 提供了更多的
　　| 轻工业的发展　|　　　| 基本建设 |

　　| 原料 |。
　　| 资金 |

二、为下列带"点"的汉字注音，并组成词组：
　　1. 调整　　强调　　协调　　失调
　　2. 重工业　　重申　　比重　　重视
　　3. 增长　　成长　　延长　　长期
　　4. 相应　　应该　　供应　　应邀

三、选词填空：
　　1. 中国国民经济经过三年多的调整，工农业等主要经济部门开始_____协调发展的新局面。（表现、出现）
　　2. 过去，由于片面强调优先发展重工业，结果造成国民经济各部门_____失调。（比重　比例）
　　3. 最近三年来，轻工业生产每年递增14%，_____速度是1952年以来最快的。（增长　增加）
　　4. 现在，轻工业部门_____出更多人民生活需要的适销对路的产品。（生产　产生）
　　5. 当前市场繁荣，食品和日用工业品_____充足。（供应　提供）
　　6. 农业和轻工业的发展_____基本建设提供了更多的资金。（为　为了）

四、熟悉下列词组：

1.
一系列	措施
	政策
	办法
	问题
	错误

2.
平均	收入
速度	
寿命	
年龄	

3.
比重	上升
	下降
	增加
	减少

4.
供应	不足
电力	
体力	
营养	

5.
稳步	增长
迅速	
大幅度	
缓慢	
逐步	
日益	
有所	

6.
提供	原料
	资金
	援助
	情报
	技术
	经验

7.
农	业
工	
轻工	
重工	
林	
牧	
副	
渔	
商	

五、阅 读

中国国民经济调整的初步成效

新华社北京8月18日电 经过三年多的调整，我国国民经济取得了更加健康的发展，人民得到了更多的实惠。目前市场繁荣，物价基本稳定，食品和日用工业品供应充足。

显示国民经济健康发展的事实包括：

——一九七九年以来，农业和轻工业加快了发展速度，重工业调整了服务方向，为国民经济各部门提供更广泛的服务。

——在农业方面，一九八一年和一九七八年相比，中国农业总产值增长了百分之十八，今年夏收小麦总产量超过去年。正在收割的早稻，一片丰收景象，秋季作物生长良好。

——这三年中轻工业增长了百分之四十八点一，今年头七个月又比去年同期增长百分之九点六。

重工业发展的速度一九八〇年比上年只增长了百分之一点四，一九八一年重工业总产值比上年降低了百分之四点七，经过调整服务方向，今年前七个月的产值比去年同期上升百分之九点七。

——国民经济的三大部门农轻重过去发展不平衡，

经过调整，现在得到更协调的发展。这是国民经济调整的主要目的之一。

——在基本建设方面，加强了与人民生活有关的非生产性建设。近三年累计，国家用于文教卫生、城市公用事业、职工住宅等人民生活方面的建设投资共四百九十三亿元，非生产性建设投资占基本建设投资总额的比重，已由一九七八年的百分之十七点四，上升到百分之四十一点二。国家增加了用于改善人民生活和职工福利的拨款，这是调整的重要内容之一。

——在外贸方面今年上半年出口额大于进口额。

(1982 年)

生　词

1. 成效　　（名）chéngxiào　　effect; result
2. 实惠　　（名、形）shíhuì　　material benefit; substantial; solid
3. 物价　　（名）wùjià　　prices
4. 显示　　（动）xiǎnshì　　show
5. 包括　　（动）bāokuò　　include
6. 夏收　　（名）xiàshōu　　summer harvest
7. 秋季　　（名）qiūjì　　autumn
8. 作物　　（名）zuòwù　　crop
9. 累计　　（动）lěijì　　accumulative total; add up

10.	文教	（名）	wénjiào	culture and education
11.	职工	（名）	zhígōng	staff and workers
12.	福利	（名）	fúlì	welfare
13.	外贸	（名）	wàimào	foreign trade

问 题

1. 中国调整国民经济的初步成效在市场上有什么表现？
2. 近三年来，中国的农业和轻工业发展如何？
3. 在调整期间，中国的重工业发展情况怎样？
4. 在基本建设方面，自调整以来有什么变化？
5. 调整的初步成效还表现在哪些方面？

第 十 二 课

一、范 句

1. 我 喜欢 包干 到户 生产 责任制，
   Wǒ xǐhuān bāogānr dào hù shēngchǎn zérènzhì
   因为 我 干 得 多 就 收入 得 多，
   yīnwéi wǒ gàn de duō jiù shōurù de duō
   而且 我 能 自由 安排 自己 的 时间。
   érqiě wǒ néng zìyóu ānpái zìjǐ de shíjiān

   I like the household resposibility system because I earn more for doing more, and I can arrange time as I like.

2. 生产 队长 和 会计 没有 办法 分清
   Shēngchǎnduìzhǎng hé kuàijì méiyǒu bànfǎ fēnqīng
   谁 干 得 多，谁 只是 走了 过场。
   shuí gàn de duō shuí zhǐshì zǒule guòchǎng

   The poduction team leader and the bookkeeper could not judge who did more and who just drifted along.

3. 社员 的 分配 是 按照 工分 计算 的，
   Shèyuán de fēnpèi shì ànzhào gōngfēnr jìsuàn de
   这 使 社员 丧失了 劳动 积极性。
   zhè shǐ shèyuán sàngshīle láodòng jījíxìng

   The income of the peasants was then based on the number of workpoints they earned, and this limited peasants' enthusiasm for work.

4. 全 国 百分 之 九十五 的 生产队 已
   Quánguó bǎifēn zhī jiǔshíwǔ de shēngchǎnduì yǐ
   实行了 各种 形式 的 生产 责任制。
   shíxíngle gèzhǒng xíngshì de shēngchǎn zérènzhì

   95 percent of the production teams in China have adopted various forms of the responsibility system.

5. 有些 地区 选择了 由 生产队 集体
   Yǒuxiē dìqū xuǎnzéle yóu shēngchǎnduì jítǐ
   经营 的 生产 责任制。
   jīngyíng de shēngchǎn zérènzhì

   Some areas have chosen collective resposibility system run by the produciton team.

6. 他们 家 向 生产队 承包了 二 点
   Tāmen jiā xiàng shēngchǎnduì chéngbāole èr diǎnr
   六 公顷 耕地。
   liù gōngqǐng gēngdì

   Their family signed a contract with the production team to farm 2.6 hectares of land.

7. 他们 每年 向 国家 交 四百 二十 二
   Tāmen měinián xiàng guójiā jiā sìbǎi èrshí èr
   公斤 公粮 即 农业税。
   gōngjīn gōngliáng jí nóngyèshuì

   Every year they delivered 422 kilograms of grain as agricultural tax in kind to the state.

8. 剩下 的 农产品 都 属于 他们 自己
   Shèngxia de nóngchǎnpǐn dōu shǔyú tāmen zìjǐ

所有， 可以 自己 留用、 储备 或 出售。
suǒyǒu kěyǐ zìjǐ liúyòng chǔbèi huò chūshòu

The remainder of the agricultural products belong to the family for its own use, storage or sale.

9. 生产 责任制 能 使 农民 直接 看到
Shēngchǎn zérènzhì néng shǐ nóngmín zhíjiē kàndào
自己 的 劳动 成果。
zìjǐ de láodòng chéngguǒ

The responsibility system of production can enable the peasants to see directly the results of their labour.

10. 现在， 他们 家 也 料理 得 更 好 了。
Xiànzài tāmen jiā yě liàolǐ de gèng hǎo le

Now they can take better care of their families.

11. 农业 生产 责任制 改变了 中国
Nóngyè shēngchǎn zérènzhì gǎibiànle Zhōngguó
农村 的 劳动 组织 形式、 经营 管理
nóngcūn de láodòng zǔzhī xíngshì jīngyíng guǎnlǐ
方式 和 劳动 计酬 办法。
fāngshì hé láodòng jìchóu bànfǎ

The responsibility system of agricultural production has changed the organization of labour and the method of management and income distribution in China's countryside.

12. 现在 是 用 经济 的 办法 即 用 合同
Xiànzài shì yòng jīngjì de bànfǎ jí yòng hétóng
的 办法 管理 农业， 而 不 是 像 过去
de bànfǎ guǎnlǐ nóngyè ér bù shì xiàng guòqù
那样 用 行政 命令 的 办法。
nàyàng yòng xíngzhèng mìnglìng de bànfǎ

It gives agricultural production guidance not through administrative directives but through economic measures, that is, through contracts.

二、课　文

中国农民喜欢农业生产责任制

新华社北京8月21日电 安徽省凤阳县大庙公社四十九岁的女社员杨守珍说:"我喜欢包干到户生产责任制,因为我现在干得多就收入得多。我能够自由安排自己的时间"。她说:"以前各种农活都是一大帮人一起干。生产队长和会计没有办法分清谁干得多,谁只是走了过场。"

过去,社员的分配是按照工分计算的,而工分是按照每个人干的农活种类和出工天数计算的,同他们的劳动数量和质量没有联系,这使社员丧失了劳动积极性。目前,全国百分之九十五的生产队已实行了各种形式的农业生产责任制。一半以上的地方实行了包干到户和包产到户责任制,农户和生产队订立了合同,在完成合同的条件下,可以按照自己的意愿自行安排各种农活。还有许多地方选择了由生产队———一般有二十至三十农户———集体经营责任制,生产队决定种植任务,安排劳动力。

杨守珍和她丈夫汤明显一家的例子说明了包干到户责任制实行的具体办法。他们家八口人向生产队承包二点六公顷耕地。按照合同他们家要向国家完成以下交售任务：每年要交四百二十二公斤公粮即农业税，并向国家卖一百三十三公斤统购粮。以上两项占他们全家每年收获粮食总产量的百分之三以上。他们还要按照规定向国家出售油料作物、烤烟、猪、蛋品。此外，他们每年要交给生产队一百三十五元一角的集体提留，供集体扩大再生产和集体福利等用，占他们收入的百分之三左右。剩下的农产品都属于他们自己所有，可以自己留用、储备或出售。

安徽农民称赞包干到户生产责任制是：既方便，又简单，直来直去不拐弯。这种办法能使农民直接看到自己的劳动成果。

许多女社员说，她们过去又要和男社员同样下地劳动，回家又要做饭带孩子，顾了这头就顾不好另外一头。现在家也料理得更好了。

包产到户和包干到户一样，以户为单位经营，但分配方法不同，生产队将产量包到户，农户向生产队交承包的产量，由生产队统一分配，超产部分归自己。

农业生产责任制改变了中国农村的劳动组织形式，经营管理方式和劳动计酬办法。

凤阳县农委副主任唐传璞说，在实行包干到户和包产到户的地方，农户的生产仍然是在国家和集体的指导下进行的。他说："过去，国家干部或生产队长每天指挥农民干什么农活和应该怎样干；现在，集体按照国家计划给农户下达任务，对农户按年度进行指导，用经济的办法即用订合同的办法管理农业，而不是像过去一样用行政命令的办法。"

(1982 年)

三、生　词

1. 社员	（名）	shèyuán	commune member
2. 包干到户		bāogānr dào hù	the household contract system of responsibility (under the unified management of the production team, each household retain evrything produced on the land assigned to it after paying taxes and contributing its share to the accumulation and public welfare funds)
3. 会计	（名）	kuàijì	accountant
4. 走过场		zǒuguòchǎng	make a gesture to give the impression of doing sth.
5. 分配	（动）	fēnpèi	distribute; assign
6. 工分	（名）	gōngfēnr	workpoint
7. 数量	（名）	shùliàng	quantity; amount
8. 质量	（名）	zhìliàng	quality
9. 合同	（名）	hétong	contract
10. 一般	（形）	yībān	general; common

11.	承包	(动) chéngbāo	contract
12.	公顷	(量) gōngqǐng	hectare
13.	统购	(动) tǒnggòu	state monopoly for purchase
14.	再生产	zàishēngchǎn	reproduction
15.	属于	(动) shǔyú	belong to
16.	储备	(动) chǔbèi	store for future use; lay up; reserve
17.	称赞	(动) chēngzàn	praise
18.	拥护	(动) yōnghù	support
19.	料理	(动) liàolǐ	arrange; take care of
20.	包产到户	bāochǎn dào hù	the system of fixing output quotas based on household
21.	计酬	jìchóu	reward counting
22.	行政命令	xíngzhèng mìnglìng	administrative decree

专　名

1.	安徽省	Ānhuī Shěng	Anhui province
2.	凤阳县	Fèngyáng Xiàn	Fengyang county
3.	大庙公社	Dàmiào Gōngshè	Damiao people's commune
4.	杨守珍	Yáng Shǒuzhēn	人名
5.	汤明显	Tāng Míngxiǎn	人名
6.	唐传璞	Táng Chuánpú	人名

Translation

Chinese Peasants like Responsibility System

Beijing, August 21 (Xinhua) — "I like the household responsibility system because I now earn more for doing more and I can arrange my time as I like," said 49-year-old Yang Shouzhen of the Damiao people's Commune in Fengyang county of Anhui province.

"Previous to this," she said, "we used to do all farm work in large groups, the production team leader and the bookkeeper could not judge who did more and who just drifted along."

Formerly the income of the peasants was then based on the number of workpoints they earned, and the workpoints were computed according to the type of work done and the days of attendence without linkage to the quantity and quality of work. This limited peasants' enthusiasm for work. At present, 95 percent of the production teams in China have adopted various forms of the responsibility system. Over half of the rural areas in China have adopted the household responsibility system and the system of fixing output quotas based on households. Under the systems, the production team sign a contract with each peasant family and the contract allows the peasant family to arrange farm work as it sees best, provided it fulfills the contract. Some areas have the collective responsibility system under which the production team, in general 20 to 30 families, decides on farm tasks and deploys the labor power.

The family of Yang Shouzhen and her husband Tang Mingxian is an example of how the household responsibility system operates. Their family of eight signed a contract with the production team to farm 2.6 hectares of land. Under the contract, it has to fulfill these obligations to the state: to deliver 422 kilograms of grain as agricultural tax in kind and sell 133 kilograms grain a year. These two items account for only a little over three percent of the family's annual grain output. The family also has to sell specified amounts of oil bearing seeds, tobacco, pork and eggs to the state according to the quota. In addition, the family hands in 135.1 yuan for the collective a year, to be used for expanding collective production, social welfare and other purposes. This accounts for three percent of the family's annual income. The remainder of the products belong to the family for its own use, storage or sale at its own discretion.

The peasants in Auhui province praise the household responsibility system as "convenient, simple and straightforward, without complicated methods." It enables the peasants to see directly the results of their labor.

Many women peasants said that formerly they had to work long hours in the fields like the men and had to do household chores and look after the children back home, and either this or that part of the work suffered. Now they can take better care of their families.

The system of "fixing output quotas based on households" is the same to the household responsibility system. It works according to the principle of household management but has a different method for income distribution. The production team fixes output quotas for each family. The family, after delivering to the team the fixed output quotas for unified income distribution by the team, keeps the rest of the harvest for itself.

The responsibility system of agricultural production has changed the organization of labor and the methods of management and income distribution in China's countryside.

Tang Chuanpu, deputy director of the Fengyang county agricultural commission, pointed out that under the household responsibility system and the system of fixing output quotas based on households the family still farms under the guidance of the collective in line with state plans. "formerly government cadres or team leaders gave the peasants daily concrete work assignments. Now the collective sets the broad outlines for the year's production for the peasant families once a year in line with state plans. It gives them guidance not through administrative directives but through economic measures, that is, through contracts." he said.

四、练 习

一、替换练习：

1. 目前，全国 [95％的生产队 / 一半以上的地方 / 有些地方] 实行了 [各种形式 / 包干到户 / 生产队集体经营] 的农业生产责任制。

2. 农民在完成 [合同 / 交售任务] 的条件下，可以按照自己的意愿 [安排各种农活 / 出售农副产品]。

3. 他们家每年要交给 [生产队 135元 / 国家 422公斤公粮] 的集体基金。

4. 现在是 [用 / 采用 / 利用] [订合同的办法 / 承包的办法 / 经济手段] 管理农业，而不是象过去那样用行政命令的办法。

二、选词填空：

　　　　由　同　向　以　把　按照

1. 过去，社员分配是____工分计算的，____他们的劳动数量和质量没有联系。
2. 杨守珍一家八口，_____生产队承包了2.6公顷耕地。
3. 他们要_____合同规定的数量、质量，_____国家出售农副产品。
4. 包产到户和包干到户一样，都是_____户为单位经营，但分配的方法不一样。
5. 包干到户的农户要_____承包数量的农产品交给生产队，_____生产队统一分配，超产部分属于自己。
6. 有些地方仍然实行_____生产队集体经营的农业生产责任制。
7. 在实行包干到户的地方，集体_____国家计划给农户下达生产任务，并进行指导，采用订合同的办法管理农业。

三、指出哪种解释符合句中划线部分词语的意思：
1. 以前各种农活大家一起干，分不清谁干得多，谁是<u>走过场</u>。
   (1) 经过场地
   (2) 表面上作了一事，而没效果。
   (3) 走过舞台表演
2. 目前，许多生产队实行了<u>包干到户</u>的农业生产责任制。
   (1) 全家人干一样的工作
   (2) 根据合同，农户承包全部生产任务
   (3) 把干部分到各家一起劳动
3. 农户每年还要交给生产队一定数量的集体基金，供集体<u>扩大再生产</u>和集体福利使用。
   (1) 进行更大规模的生产
   (2) 继续大量生产
   (3) 加紧重复生产

4. 完成承包任务外，超产部分归自己。
   (1) 自己取回来
   (2) 属于自己
   (3) 还给自己

四、熟悉下列词组：

1. | 农业生产 | 责任制 |
包干到户	
包产到户	
企业管理	
经济	

2. | 安排 | 时间 |
	农活
	工作
	活动
	生活

3. | 完成 | 任务 |
	工作
	计划
	工程

4. | 集体 | 经营 |
	福利
	企业
	活动
	婚礼

5. | 公 | 粮 |
统购	
商品	
救济	
余	

6. | 劳动 | 数量 |
	质量
	成果
	组织形式
	计酬办法
	生产率

五、阅 读

农业生产责任制
改善了贫困地区农民的生活

新华社北京8月21日电 过去缺粮的安徽省凤阳县今夏获得小麦大丰收,估计总产量达十五万吨,一季小麦的产量足够全县五十万农村人口吃一年。

这是自从一九七九年实行农业生产责任制以来,凤阳县连续第四年取得小麦丰收,今年的小麦产量又超过了去年。凤阳是全国实行包干到户责任制最早的县分之一。

解放前,凤阳的农民由于贫困每年大批出外逃荒。凤阳县今年的夏收小麦超过了一九七八年全年粮食的产量,丰收的小麦堆放在农民住房附近,而许多农民家里留下来的存粮还够吃好几个月。

实行农业生产责任制后,农民的生产积极性提高了,施用更多的化肥和改进耕作方法,产量提高了。小麦、玉米已成为那里农民的主食。农民手里有了余粮又有了自由支配的时间,就可以饲养更多的家畜、家禽,这些家庭副业也增加了他们的家庭收入。

农民们充满了丰收的喜悦。安徽省凤阳县大庙公社社员杨锦礼说:"我要卖余粮和烟叶,准备盖砖瓦房和购买化肥。"其他农民说，他们卖了余粮后，准备买自行车或给儿子办喜事，还有许多农民计划买农具和大牲畜扩大再生产。中国农民今年上半年购买的化肥比去年同期增加百分之八，购买的小农具数量也增加了。许多地方，小农具已供不应求。

在凤阳县，副县长王昌泰说：几乎全县所有的农民收入都增加了。有充足劳动力的家庭和有种田能手、家庭副业能手的家庭，收入比其他家庭增长得更快。王昌泰说，这是实行社会主义按劳分配原则的必然结果。每个人都按劳取酬，并没有出现人剥削人的现象。

王昌泰说，由于整个农村经济水平的提高，集体现在有了更多的公积金和公益金，可以从公益金中提取更多的款项给予五保户更好的照顾。除了五保户之外，农村还有一些其他的困难户，这主要是子女多、缺乏劳动力的家庭和偶然遭到病、丧等不幸的家庭。副县长王昌泰说，这些困难户只占全县农户总数的百分之几，比例比过去大大减少，政府已采取措施给予经济和技术上的帮助。

凤阳县带头实行包干到户的严洪昌在回顾几年来的发展时说，"我很高兴现在我们不再靠国家救济，每年能卖余粮，为社会主义做出一点贡献，社会主义给我们带来美好的生活，我绝不背离社会主义道路。我们农民想要摆脱的是干好干坏一个样的平均主义。"

(1982 年)

生 词

1. 估计 （动） gūjì — estimate; appraise; reckon
2. 逃荒 táohuāng — flee from famine
3. 化肥 （名） huàféi — chemical fertilizer
4. 耕作 （动） gēngzuò — cultivate; farm
5. 饲养 （动） sìyǎng — raise; rear
6. 余粮 （名） yúliáng — surplus grain
7. 大牲畜 （名） dàshēngchù — draught animal
8. 能手 （名） néngshǒu — dab; expert
9. 按劳分配 àn láo fēnpèi — distribution according to work
10. 剥削 （动） bōxuē — exploit
11. 公积金 （名） gōngjījīn — accumulation fund (of a socialist economic collective)
12. 公益金 （名） gōngyìjīn — public welfare fund
13. 五保户 （名） wǔbǎohù — a household enjoying the five guarantees (childless and infirm old persons who are guaranteed food, clothing, medical care, housing and burial expenses by the people's commune)
14. 照顾 （动） zhàogù — look after; care for
15. 事故 （名） shìgù — accident

16. 救济	（动）	jiùjì	relieve
17. 摆脱	（动）	bǎituō	cast off; shake off
18. 平均主义	（名）	píngjūn zhǔyì	equalitarianism; egalitarianism

专 名

1. 杨锦礼　　Yáng Jǐnlǐ　　人名
2. 王昌泰　　Wáng Chāngtài　　人名
3. 严洪昌　　Yán Hóngchāng　　人名

问 题

1. 安徽省凤阳县今年夏收情况怎样？
2. 这个地区农民的生活有什么变化？
3. 小麦丰收的原因有哪些？
4. 丰收以后，农民们有什么打算？
5. 什么样的家庭变化最大、最快？
6. 什么样的家庭生活上还有困难？怎么解决？
7. 带头实行包干到户的严洪昌是怎样想的？

词 汇 表

词后的数字表示课数，有括号的表示该课阅读部分的生词

A

爱好	àihào	4
安居乐业	ānjūlèyè	10
安排	ānpái	5
安置	ānzhì	9
按劳分配	ànláofēnpèi	(12)

B

摆脱	bǎituō	(12)
搬运	bānyùn	(9)
邦交	bāngjiāo	2
包产到户	bāochǎndàohù	12
包干到户	bāogànrdàohù	12
包括	bāokuò	(11)
保持	bǎochí	3
保留	bǎoliú	5
保证	bǎozhèng	5
暴行	bàoxíng	4
卑贱	bēijiàn	(10)
比例	bǐlì	2
比重	bǐzhòng	11

毕业生	bìyèshēng	(9)
避孕	bìyùn	8
辩论	biànlùn	(4)
表决	biǎojué	(6)
剥削	bōxuē	(12)
补助	bǔzhù	5
不妨	bùfāng	(5)
不失为	bùshīwéi	(5)
不幸	bùxìng	5
部署	bùshǔ	(4)
步骤	bùzhòu	(3)

C

财产	cáichǎn	5
财政	cáizhèng	5
采取	cǎiqǔ	4
参与	cānyù	5
曾	céng	1
层次	céngcì	7
阐明	chǎnmíng	5
常识	chángshí	7
敞开	chǎngkāi	11

彻底	chèdǐ	(3)	当局	dāngjú	4
称赞	chēngzàn	12	灯火辉煌	dēnghuǒhuīhuáng	
承包	chéngbāo	12			(6)
承认	chéngrèn	3	电子	diànzǐ	(9)
呈现	chéngxiàn	7	堤防	dīfáng	(5)
成效	chéngxiào	(11)	抵达	dǐdá	(1)
城镇	chéngzhèn	9	地利	dìlì	(2)
充分	chōngfèn	5	第一把手	dìyībǎshǒu	10
冲击	chōngjī	(5)	第一线	dìyīxiàn	2
重申	chóngshēn	2	递增	dìzēng	11
出生率	chūshēnglǜ	(8)	叮咛	dīngníng	(5)
出席	chūxí	1	定居	dìngjū	5
储备	chǔbèi	12	定心丸	dìngxīnwán	(5)
从事	cóngshì	2	独立	dúlì	4
磋商	cuōshāng	(4)	独生子女	dúshēngzǐnǚ	(8)
措施	cuòshī	4	对待	duìdài	(3)
			对方	duìfāng	3

D

F

达成	dáchéng	3			
大幅度	dàfúdù	10	发表	fābiǎo	(3)
大牲畜	dàshēngchù	(12)	发言人	fāyánrén	4
大使	dàshǐ	1	翻一番	fānyīfān	7
大使馆	dàshǐguǎn	3	繁荣	fánróng	11
大业	dàyè	5	范围	fànwéi	3
代销店	dàixiāodiàn	(9)	放宽	fàngkuān	10
待业	dàiyè	9	放映	fàngyìng	(5)
担任	dānrèn	2	分布	fēnbù	(9)
诞生	dànshēng	(6)	分裂	fēnliè	5

分配	fēnpèi	12		公布	gōngbù	3
分析	fēnxī	7		公积金	gōngjījīn	(12)
风俗	fēngsú	10		公顷	gōngqǐng	12
封建思想	fēngjiàn sīxiǎng	8		公司	gōngsī	9
夫人	fūrén	1		公益金	gōngyìjīn	(12)
符合	fúhé	3		供不应求	gōngbùyìngqiú	(9)
福利	fúlì	(11)		供应	gōngyìng	8
妇联	fùlián	8		共青团	gòngqīngtuán	8
副部长	fùbùzhǎng	1		贡献	gòngxiàn	2
副食品	fùshípǐn	11		估计	gūjì	(12)
副业	fùyè	11		鼓励	gǔlì	9
负责	fùzé	9		官方	guānfāng	3
				关键	guānjiàn	(3)
G				观察员	guāncháyuán	(4)
概括	gàikuò	2		管理	guǎnlǐ	5
概念	gàiniàn	7		贯彻	guànchè	9
干涉	gānshè	(3)		规划	guīhuà	7
干预	gānyù	5		贵宾	guìbīn	1
高级官员	gāojí guānyuán	(1)		国策	guócè	2
高涨	gāozhǎng	6		国歌	guógē	1
隔绝	géjué	(5)		国际	guójì	2
各界	gèjiè	2		国民经济	guómín jīngjì	11
个体	gètǐ	9		国是	guóshì	5
耕作	gēngzuò	(12)		国事访问	guóshì fǎngwèn	1
工程师	gōngchéngshī	(10)		国务委员	guówù wěiyuán	1
工分	gōngfēnr	12		国营	guóyíng	9
工会	gōnghuì	8				
工商界	gōngshāngjiè	5		**H**		

海内外	hǎinèiwài	(5)		纪念	jìniàn	2
海峡	hǎixiá	5		加工	jiāgōng	(9)
函授	hánshòu	7		家禽	jiāqín	11
悍然	hànrán	4		兼	jiān	1
行业	hángyè	9		监票人	jiānpiàorén	(6)
号召	hàozhào	9		简便	jiǎnbiàn	8
核对	héduì	(6)		减少	jiǎnshǎo	3
合法	héfǎ	3		检阅	jiǎnyuè	1
合同	hétong	12		建交	jiànjiāo	(1)
和平事业	hépíng shìyè	3		建议	jiànyì	5
呼声	hūshēng	10		教育	jiàoyù	7
互通音讯	hùtōng yīnxùn	5		接触	jiēchù	5
化肥	huàféi	(12)		结构	jiégòu	7
恢复	huīfù	(4)		节育	jiéyù	8
会见	huìjiàn	2		解释	jiěshì	(7)
				届	jiè	2

J

				紧急	jǐnjí	(4)
基本建设	jīběn jiànshè	11		锦绣山河	jǐnxiù shānhé	(5)
基督教	Jīdūjiào	(4)		进而	jìnér	4
机构	jīgòu	5		经营	jīngyíng	9
即	jí	3		就	jiù	2
集体	jítǐ	9		就任	jiùrèn	(1)
集团	jítuán	3		就业	jiùyè	9
给予	jǐyǔ	10		救济	jiùjǐ	(12)
计酬	jìchóu	12		局面	júmiàn	(7)
计划生育	jìhuà shēngyù	8		决定	juédìng	3
继承	jìchéng	6		决议	juéyì	4
继承权	jìchéngquán	5		军队	jūnduì	5

军事冲突	jūnshì chōngtū	3
军乐队	jūnyuèduì	1

K

开幕	kāimù	6
开辟	kāipì	(9)
考察	kǎochá	(7)
考虑	kǎolǜ	(4)
渴望	kěwàng	(5)
控制	kòngzhì	8
会计	kuàijì	12
宽厚	kuānhòu	(5)
款待	kuǎndài	(2)
矿工	kuànggōng	(10)

L

雷鸣	léimíng	(6)
累计	lěijì	(11)
立即	lìjí	4
利润	lìrùn	5
利益	lìyì	3
联合公报	liánhé gōngbào	3
连续性	liánxùxìng	2
谅解	liàngjiě	3
料理	liàolǐ	12
列举	lièjǔ	10
邻邦	línbāng	1
临时性	línshíxìng	9

林业	línyè	11
凌晨	língchén	(4)
灵活性	línghuóxìng	(7)
领土	lǐngtǔ	(3)
隆重	lóngzhòng	1
履行	lǚxíng	(3)
绿化	lǜhuà	(9)
落后	luòhòu	7

M

蛮横	mánhèng	4
盲目	mángmù	7
门路	ménlù	9
门市部	ménshìbù	(9)
密度	mìdù	(7)
秘书长	mìshūzhǎng	4
免除	miǎnchú	10
免费	miǎnfèi	10
面临	miànlín	(5)
灭绝人性	mièjué rénxìng	4
蔑视	mièshì	4
民兵	mínbīng	(4)
民众团体	mínzhòng tuántǐ	5
名誉主席	míngyù zhǔxí	(10)
命运	mìngyùn	10
谋求	móuqiú	3
目标	mùbiāo	8
牧业	mùyè	11

N

纳粹	Nàcuì	(4)
内地	nèidì	(10)
内阁	nèigé	(2)
内政	nèizhèng	(3)
能手	néngshǒu	(12)
能源	néngyuán	(7)
农奴制	nóngnúzhì	(10)
农业	nóngyè	11
扭转	niǔzhuǎn	7

P

拍摄	pāishè	(5)
派	pài	3
陪同	péitóng	1
培训	péixùn	(9)
片面	piànmiàn	11
平均主义	píngjūnzhǔyì	12
凭票供应	píng piào gōngyìng	11
迫切	pòqiè	5
迫使	pòshǐ	4
普及	pǔjí	8

Q

歧视	qíshì	5
企业	qǐyè	9
气氛	qìfēn	(6)
弃权	qìquán	(6)
前首相	qiánshǒuxiàng	2
谴责	qiǎnzé	4
强调	qiángdiào	3
强烈	qiángliè	4
亲人团聚	qīnrén tuánjù	5
侵占	qīnzhàn	4
轻工业	qīnggōngyè	11
倾听	qīngtīng	10
秋季	qiūjì	(11)
渠道	qúdào	5
全国性	quánguóxìng	5
全民所有制	quánmín suǒyǒuzhì	9
全文	quánwén	3
权利	quánlì	4
权益	quányì	5
确保	quèbǎo	(4)
确认	quèrèn	2
群众	qúnzhòng	1

R

热诚	rèchéng	5
人才	réncái	7
人和	rénhé	(2)
人均收入	rénjūn shōurù	10

人口普查	rénkǒu pǔchá	(8)		世世代代	shìshìdàidài	2
人士	rénshì	2		事故	shìgù	(12)
容许	róngxǔ	4		事件	shìjiàn	(3)
若干	ruògān	(8)		事实	shìshí	10
				事务	shìwù	5

S

				事业单位	shìyè dānwèi	9
扫盲	sǎománg	(7)		适销对路	shìxiāo duìlù	11
商定	shāngdìng	3		适应	shìyìng	6
商务	shāngwù	3		试点	shìdiǎn	7
上将	shàngjiàng	1		收购	shōugòu	10
上述	shàngshù	4		首相	shǒuxiàng	2
少先队员	shàoxiānduìyuán	1		寿命	shòumìng	(8)
社会	shèhuì	5		属于	shǔyú	12
社员	shèyuán	12		数量	shùliàng	12
深造	shēnzào	(10)		税	shuì	10
慎重	shènzhòng	6		司机	sījī	(10)
生活方式	shēnghuófāngshì	5		私人	sīrén	5
生理	shēnglǐ	8		死亡率	sǐwánglù	(8)
声明	shēngmíng	(3)		四项基本原则		
师范	shīfàn	7			sìxiàng jīběn	
失调	shītiáo	11			yuánzé	6
实地	shídì	(7)		饲养	sìyǎng	(12)
实惠	shíhuì	(11)		速度	sùdù	11
实施	shíshī	(4)		随同	suítóng	1
实体	shítǐ	(3)		所有权	suǒyǒuquán	5
拾遗补缺	shíyíbǔquē	(9)		所有制	suǒyǒuzhì	9
市场	shìchǎng	11				
世纪	shìjì	(8)				

T

态度	tàidù	7		外交部长	wàijiāo bùzhǎng	1
谈判	tánpàn	3		外交关系	wàijiāo guānxì	3
逃荒	táohuāng	(12)		外贸	wàimào	(11)
特别行政区				外务大臣	wàiwù dàchén	2
	tèbié xíngzhèngqū	5		完整	wánzhěng	(3)
特色	tèsè	6		违反	wéifǎn	(3)
提倡	tíchàng	8		维护	wéihù	4
提供	tígōng	(2)		维修	wéixiū	(9)
提前	tíqián	3		唯一	wéiyī	3
天时	tiānshí	(2)		文化	wénhuà	3
调整	tiáozhěng	11		文教	wénjiào	(11)
通过	tōngguò	4		稳定	wěndìng	(2)
通航	tōngháng	5		无辜	wúgū	4
通商	tōngshāng	5		无记名投票	wújìmíng tóupiào	
通邮	tōngyóu	5				(6)
统购	tǒnggòu	12		无条件	wútiáojiàn	4
统计	tǒngjì	9		五保户	wǔbǎohù	(12)
统计局	tǒngjìjú	(8)		武器	wǔqì	(3)
统一	tǒngyī	(3)		物价	wùjià	(11)
统治	tǒngzhì	(10)				
投资	tóuzī	5			**X**	
突出	tūchū	8		吸取	xīqǔ	6
突破	tūpò	(5)		喜气洋洋	xǐqìyángyáng	(6)
屠杀	túshā	4		下列	xiàliè	7
推动	tuīdòng	(1)		夏收	xiàshōu	(11)
妥协	tuǒxié	(5)		显示	xiǎnshì	(11)
				县	xiàn	(9)
	W			宪法	xiànfǎ	6

182

现实	xiànshí	6		一般	yībān	12
现行	xiànxíng	6		一贯	yīguàn	2
陷于	xiànyú	5		一胎率	yītāilǜ	8
相应	xiāngyìng	11		一系列	yīxìliè	11
享受	xiǎngshòu	10		一致	yīzhì	(2)
享有	xiǎngyǒu	5		医疗	yīliáo	10
协调	xiétiáo	11		仪式	yíshì	1
协议	xiéyì	3		仪仗队	yízhàngduì	1
新闻	xīnwén	8		亿	yì	8
信仰	xìnyǎng	10		议案	yì'àn	(6)
兴办	xīngbàn	5		意味	yìwèi	(8)
行使	xíngshǐ	10		意义	yìyì	2
行政命令	xíngzhèng mìnglìng	12		因素	yīnsù	(8)
				阴影	yīnyǐng	(3)
修旧利废	xiūjiùlìfèi	(9)		应…邀请	yìng…yāoqǐng	1
修理	xiūlǐ	(9)		优待	yōudài	10
序言	xùyán	(6)		优生	yōushēng	8
宣传	xuānchuán	(5)		有助于	yǒuzhùyú	3
选举	xuǎnjǔ	10		幼儿托育	yòuér tuōyù	(9)
学术	xuéshù	5		拥护	yōnghù	12
学制	xuézhì	7		涌现	yǒngxiàn	(10)
血腥	xuèxīng	4		余粮	yúliáng	(12)
训练	xùnliàn	9		渔业	yúyè	11
训练班	xùnliànbān	(10)		与日俱增	yǔrìjùzēng	(5)
				育龄	yùlíng	(8)

Y

洋溢	yángyì	(6)				
野蛮	yěmán	4		再生产	zàishēngchǎn	12

Z

在座	zàizuò	2
责	zé	5
占	zhàn	2
招收	zhāoshōu	7
照顾	zhàogù	(12)
针对	zhēnduì	3
正常	zhèngcháng	(3)
正常化	zhèngchánghuà	2
正式	zhèngshì	(1)
正义	zhèngyì	4
政府	zhèngfǔ	1
支柱	zhīzhù	(2)
知识分子	zhīshifènzǐ	6
值得	zhídé	2
执行	zhíxíng	4
执行主席	zhíxíng zhǔxí	(6)
职工	zhígōng	(11)
职务	zhíwù	(10)
制定	zhìdìng	2
制度	zhìdù	5
制止	zhìzhǐ	4
智慧	zhìhuì	6
质量	zhìliàng	12
至于	zhìyú	3
衷心	zhōngxīn	(2)
中央委员会	zhōngyāng wěiyuánhuì	2
重工业	zhònggōngyè	11
众所周知	zhòngsuǒzhōuzhī	(3)
周到	zhōudào	6
周年	zhōunián	2
主持	zhǔchí	1
主权	zhǔquán	(3)
驻	zhù	1
祝贺	zhùhè	2
专机	zhuānjī	1
转达	zhuǎndá	(2)
转化	zhuǎnhuà	7
庄严	zhuāngyán	(6)
状态	zhuàngtài	(3)
准则	zhǔnzé	4
酌情	zhuóqíng	5
资金	zījīn	11
资源	zīyuán	7
自负盈亏	zìfùyíngkuī	(9)
自然增长率	zìrán zēngzhǎnglǜ	(8)
自治区	zìzhìqū	9
自治权	zìzhìquán	5
宗教	zōngjiào	10
总产量	zǒngchǎnliàng	10
总产值	zǒngchǎnzhí	10
总理大臣	zǒnglǐ dàchén	2
总统	zǒngtǒng	1
走过场	zǒuguòchǎng	12

奏	zòu	1	尊重	zūnzhòng	（3）
组织	zǔzhī	9	作物	zuòwù	（11）
罪行	zuìxíng	4			